ALSO BY DR. CAROLYN EDWARDS

Illustrated by Gabrielle Liedtke

Books to help children learn and navigate life

I Can Be Anything I Dream

Fun With Money

10 Simple Steps to Get Your Résumé Noticed
and Land the Job

Teach ONLINE

DR. CAROLYN EDWARDS

BALBOA.
PRESS

A DIVISION OF HAY HOUSE

Balboa Press books may be ordered through booksellers or by contacting:

Balboa Press
A Division of Hay House
1663 Liberty Drive
Bloomington, IN 47403
www.balboapress.com
1-(877) 407-4847

Because of the dynamic nature of the Internet, any web addresses or links contained in this book may have changed since publication and may no longer be valid. The views expressed in this work are solely those of the author and do not necessarily reflect the views of the publisher, and the publisher hereby disclaims any responsibility for them.

The author of this book does not dispense medical advice or prescribe the use of any technique as a form of treatment for physical, emotional, or medical problems without the advice of a physician, either directly or indirectly. The intent of the author is only to offer information of a general nature to help you in your quest for emotional and spiritual well-being. In the event you use any of the information in this book for yourself, which is your constitutional right, the author and the publisher assume no responsibility for your actions.

Any people depicted in stock imagery provided by Thinkstock are models, and such images are being used for illustrative purposes only.
Certain stock imagery © Thinkstock.

ISBN: 978-1-4525-4915-6 (sc)
ISBN: 978-1-4525-4916-3 (hc)
ISBN: 978-1-4525-4914-9 (e)

Library of Congress Control Number: 2012905607

Printed in the United States of America

Balboa Press rev. date: 05/01/2012

Dedication

---◆·▪·◆---

For my husband and son who always give me the love and support needed to navigate my destiny and to everyone with the courage to live their dreams.

*If one advances confidently in the direction of his dreams,
and endeavors to live the life which he has imagined, he will
meet with a success unexpected in common hours.*
- Henry David Thoreau

It's time to start living the life you imagined.
— Henry James

Contents

PART ONE: FUNDAMENTALS

PART TWO: PREPARATION

PART THREE: LAND THE JOB

Acknowledgments

———◦✦◦———

Everything in my life has been accomplished with faith and trust in God, which led me to the right people who ushered this book into print. For that I am extremely grateful.

I particularly wish to thank my parents Agnes and Johnny and grandparents Granny and CeeCee for providing the foundation that reassured me that I could help others and live my dreams. To all my family, friends, ancestors, and loved ones who encouraged me, I could not have done it without you.

To those who shared your stories through online blogs, emails, and surveys, your experiences will help others to achieve their dreams. Thanks for inspiring me to include them in this book.

For all of my nieces and nephews, may you always know that you can do anything you set your mind to just by being yourselves and doing what you love. Remember that you have many talents, so pursue your lives with passion. I love you all. Thank you to my Edwards family for your love, support and warm welcome.

Thanks as well to Marc D. Baldwin, Ph.D., and the staff of Edit911. com, Inc. for editing my doctoral dissertation.

Miami Women of Color Book Club, thanks for welcoming me to Florida and allowing me to exhale while discussing not only books but also life.

To my son Jeremiah, who served as my muse, keep on dancing and let your light continue to shine.

Finally, I thank my husband for his love, encouragement, and critiques but especially for not cleaning my office even when the stacks of research materials were driving him crazy.

Introduction

Every day do one thing to move you in the direction of your dreams. — Dr. Carolyn Edwards

You are today where your thoughts have brought you; you will be tomorrow where your thoughts take you. — James Allen

Over the past ten or so years I have received a multitude of inquiries from people wanting to know how I landed an online teaching job. It took so much time to answer each inquiry that I decided to write down not only my story but also the stories of others successfully teaching online. Although there is no particular secret, online teaching still eludes the vast majority of those who apply for such assignments. Many believe that they are not doing something right or that they don't have access to the right information or people. This book presents ten simple steps to help you find online teaching opportunities; get your résumé noticed by recruiters and land the job. You learn not only how to teach online but also how to educate online, which opens up a great deal more opportunities. Just changing the word from "teaching" to "educating" will give you access to jobs in which you can facilitate, develop, and deliver educational content.

Information Awaits You

The information you need is already out there. If you put the energy and effort into making your dream of teaching online come true, you can indeed land such a job. However, there is a way to work smart, a way to get the inside track, a way to demonstrate your value to an organization. Be ready and willing to do the work. Invest in yourself, and don't forget to do your homework.

The idea of teaching online is so much more than what you think and so much broader than what it was just a few years ago. The industry today encompasses a lot of opportunities not only to teach but also to educate. This means that you can teach, lecture, facilitate, coach, and develop curriculum while working online at home. To help you focus on the abundance of opportunities available, I will use a variety of words such as "educate," "instruct," "facilitate," "develop," and "teach online" throughout the book. These terms are used in the various job descriptions and you need to cast your net wide to get the best results. That means you should look for not only online teaching jobs but also the plethora of jobs involving online education. I want you to you know that there are many opportunities to do what you love, and reading this book will help you to take advantage of them.

The Right Stuff

When you apply for a position, the goal should always be to demonstrate how you can help an organization to achieve its mission and goals. If I could give a single tip, it would be that when you apply for a job take the focus off you and shift it to how the organization can win by using you as an educator. Let me say it a different way. How can students succeed by having you as the instructor, designer, facilitator, or teacher? Answering this question will help you to develop a successful résumé and cover letter.

Revising your application to address the requirements of the job takes a shift in thinking. When applying for a position, job seekers often think about their needs, wants, or desires, but those of the employer must be detailed in your application. Taking your ego out of the equation and focusing on the organization's needs is the first step in becoming more effective at landing a job.

Many of you may be thinking, "It's easy for her to say that there are jobs out there because she already has a doctorate," but that is not quite the case. When I first started teaching, I didn't have a Ph.D. or any experience as a college instructor, but what I did have was faith in my abilities to help students succeed.

It doesn't matter whether you have a Ph.D., Ed.D., J.D., or master's degree. It doesn't matter whether you have twenty years of experience or none at all. With that in mind, I nonetheless continue to get asked the same questions:

- Can you help me get an online job?

- I don't know where to begin. Can you point me in the right direction?

- Can you review my résumé?

This book tells not only my story but also the stories of those successfully educating online and working from the comfort of home or anywhere in the world that has an Internet connection. You will read about those who didn't have any teaching or online facilitation experience but who still were able to use common strategies such as networking and volunteering to land an online teaching job. It happens more often than you might think, when you know where to look and have the necessary tools.

My Story

For the past eleven years I have been an online professor. My journey started with a wish and a dream. I was not trained as a teacher, my background being in information technology, programming, network administration, and computer auditing. My master's degree is in management. Consequently, my day-to-day duties involved managing information-technology programs for a federal government agency. The agency where I worked allowed us one hour each week to do community service at an inner-city school adopted by the agency. I served as a teacher's assistant with a colleague helping students with lessons developed by the Junior Achievement program.

After spending weeks working on curriculum development and creating tools to help students learn, I was hooked. I loved teaching so much that my coworker left all the planning and development of student activities to me. She delivered the lessons, but the creative part was all mine, and I loved it. Conducting the research, finding helpful tools, and seeing students understand the lessons fueled an inner passion. This was more exciting than the work I did forty plus hours per week for the government. I knew a change had to come.

Finding a way to teach became an important goal. The switch to teaching was a very organic process. In order to be successful in educating online, make sure that it is something to which you want to commit. Passion will help to keep you motivated during the search process. Included in this book is a checklist to determine whether educating others online is right for you.

MIND SHIFT

Although I loved teaching, I knew that elementary-school age children were not my target audience. I had done some initial investigating to find out the requirements for becoming a secondary-school teacher and was not excited about that route. I would have had to take quite a few additional courses as well as earn state certification. Upon further investigation I found that many colleges required only a postsecondary degree (e.g., bachelor's or master's degree) and eighteen credit hours in the subject area. I had that number of hours in business and management, thirteen years of professional experience, and lots of expertise in using technology, all of which helped my job applications to stand out.

For many schools, especially four-year institutions, a master's degree and eighteen credit hours in the subject matter is the minimum requirement for online teaching. However, that's not to say there aren't special cases or schools/organizations where you can educate others with only a bachelor's degree, though additional certification such as Certified Public Accountant (CPA), Certified Information Systems Auditor (CISA), or Licensed Practical Nurse (LPN) may be mandated. Always make sure you know the minimum job requirements for the position you're interested in getting.

While attending a networking event for the District of Columbia Chamber of Commerce, I decided to step outside my comfort zone and discuss not simply my current job but also my dream of teaching at the college level. Similarly, it may be time for you to change your way of thinking. You *can* work full-time online from home, contrary to popular belief. Think differently to achieve different results. Tell people what you want to accomplish. You never know who may be able to help you on the journey of landing an online teaching job.

For example, when I revealed to an employee of the Chamber of Commerce that I wanted to teach on the college level, he told me about a colleague, put me in touch with her, and the rest is history. The referral helped me to get my foot in the door. I received my first on-site teaching assignment within a month of placing a call to the dean. It was at a two-year career school and that was how I earned the experience that helped me land my first online teaching job.

I taught at the school for a few years and loved it so much that I wanted to teach at the graduate level and make it a career. I looked into doctoral programs, applied, and was accepted. I was commuting thirty miles each way to teach classes, the time wasted in rush-hour traffic was not conducive to study and research in my Ph.D. program. I needed more time and flexibility to complete course requirements. Furthermore, after working in corporate America for thirteen years, I was tired of spending money on dress shoes, stockings, suits, and coats when I preferred to live in a warm climate year around and wear sundresses, bright colors, and sandals most of the year.

Spending less time on the road and more time with my husband was also an important factor in my decision to teach online. When we started a family, I wanted to be able to witness all of my child's developmental milestones. Working from home would allow me to do just that. Then, while searching on the Internet for "online professor jobs," I came across various online schools with openings in the business and management areas and decided to apply to several of them. It was as simple as that. I didn't know anyone at an online school or anyone who was teaching online for that matter. What I did have was desire, passion, education, experience, and faith in my abilities.

BELIEF

I believed in my ability to land an online job. Since I had experience with information technology and a persistent personality, I was not afraid of being told no. To me being told no just meant not at this time or not at this school. To be honest, not everyone believed in my ability to earn a living by teaching online and using it as a stepping stone to move to a warmer climate, but I believed in my dream. So should you. The benefits of teaching online are awesome. I had the flexibility to care for my son at home and not have to pay for daycare. I was able to sit by the pool and work while doing something I loved.

When others tell me their apprehensions about educating online, I say that I am in my forties, that most likely half of my life is over, and that I want to use my remaining time on Earth to live my dreams. So I ask these people, "What do you want the other half of your life to look like? Do you want to make a living doing something you love, with the flexibility to work anywhere in the world, or do you want to let others dictate your career, work environment, and life? Why not start living today as if it were your last and take a chance on living your dreams?"

Ty Howard once said, "You might be delayed but not denied." Those words have stuck with me throughout my career and keep me going to this day. Persistence pays off. Prospective employers' staffing changes all the time. The department chair who rejected your application two months ago may no longer be there, or the manager who only glanced at your qualifications six months ago may now be in a different position, so keep on applying. A school where I currently teach called me after submitting my initial résumé over two years ago because I had kept applying as well as updating my credentials on their online human-resource system. I had always wanted to teach for this school and knew one day it would happen. Patience and persistence were the key! Sometimes you might have to set up an account and put your applicant documents online at the organization's site, but that's okay. Putting your credentials on their site is just one more way to keep your name in the forefront.

Know what you want, believe you can have it, and see yourself doing it. What I've accomplished you can too! Just keep taking action each day to get you there. Don't worry about how it will happen; just make the effort. As Mike Dooley says, "All we have to do is to define whatever it is we want or the changes we wish to experience in terms of the end result." If you are expecting miracles to happen without your doing any work, think again. You can realize your dreams by believing in yourself, visualizing yourself doing what you want, and then taking action to move you toward your goal. It's as simple as that.

There are many avenues and tips to get you where you want to be—namely, educating online. With the ten steps presented in this book you have the information to get you there. As Bob Proctor recommends, "Visualize what you want in as much detail as you possibly can and let that image and energy guide you to the situations and circumstances that allow you to obtain the job you seek."

READ AND ACHIEVE

Although educating online is a widely discussed subject, you'd be hard pressed to find some clear, effective, and proven step-by-step guidelines that can help you land a job. This book provides answers to the most frequently asked questions as well as strategies for success. The book is based on my eleven years of successfully educating online, experience as a consultant, research studies, and factual accounts by those currently educating online. Once you know the rules and have the tools, begin to see yourself performing the online job you desire and getting paid for it. Then go about making your dream of educating online come true.

TRUST YOURSELF

I'm writing this book because I want to help you secure an online teaching job. There are many jobs available, but many people don't believe they can land them. Remember that the information is out there. You just need to know where to look. Remember too that there's no particular secret, but there are rules, tools, tips, suggestions, resources, and action steps you can take to get a job teaching online.

Here's a word of caution: don't let someone's lack of success or the word "no" deter you from achieving your dream. Trust in the journey even when it doesn't look as though it is working in your favor. Don't be discouraged. As Robert Ringer remarked, "When your mind believes something to be true, it stimulates your senses to draw the things, people, and circumstances necessary to convert the mental image it houses into physical reality." There are thousands of online opportunities out there and lots of organizations hiring for online positions. You just need to know where to look and when. Then be ready to seize the opportunities by submitting a winning application package. Take one action each day to move you in the direction of your dream.

Warning. There are quite a few blogs and online groups that give advice about teaching online, but I suggest taking advice only from those individuals who have obtained what you seek. If the person giving advice has not received frequent course assignments or provides negative comments, keep it moving. Share your thoughts, goals, and ideas with those willing to help you succeed. Do the work, think outside the box, and prepare to get the job.

Book Basics

The beginning of the book will give you the basics to position yourself for the online job you seek. Each chapter provides an enlightening and empowering quotation to keep you focused and motivated on your journey to securing an online teaching job. At the end of each chapter is a summary you can use to develop action steps for propelling you onward. There is also space to write out your goals and action steps. Remember, above all, to take action! Dale Carnegie said, "The successful man will profit from his mistakes and try again in a different way." Don't continue to do what you've been doing and expect different results. Give the steps in this book a try.

The information presented is based on tried and proven steps, rules, practices, tools, and tips to help you get results. Scholarly research, practical application, and the personal journeys of people who are making money while educating online are the foundation of this book. These ideas and suggestions have been used by developers, teachers, writers, professors, instructors, consultants, and facilitators. You also will get tools and resources to help you think outside the box to find work in curriculum development, administration, and consulting online. Move beyond your fears to achieve your desires.

The reference section at the end provides a wealth of additional information such as online job sites, résumé samples, and other resources. The people included in this book were kind enough to share their experiences to help you be successful. Think about what you want to achieve and see yourself making money by educating online. Surround yourself with helpful people and opportunities that can get you moving in the right direction.

Terms like "brick-and-mortar" or "on-site," finally, will be used to denote face-to-face instruction or organizations with physical instructional facilities, as opposed to online learning conducted via the Internet or World Wide Web.

Stop Making Excuses

The steps presented in this book work! You have the power to live the life you want. In support for that claim, I offer the following true story.

A dear friend of mine had spent two years at an accounting firm commuting three hours back and forth to work each day. When traffic was bad, she would be unavoidably late in picking up her son from daycare. The center charged an extra five dollars for every minute she was late. Needless to say, two years of such a long daily commute made her frustrated, tired, and broke. I shared with her the steps in this book. She was skeptical at first because she didn't have any prior teaching experience. I promised her that if she tried the steps for at least one year and didn't get at least one online assignment, I would give her $100.

Within six months she had an online assignment. She now works full-time from home with an increase in pay developing curriculum and teaching accounting classes. Not only does she have employee benefits of health, life, and dental insurance, but she also has lost twenty pounds because she no longer eats in the car while stuck in traffic. She now has time to volunteer at her son's school during the day and has saved quite a nest egg for his college education.

This can be your story. Change your mind and behavior to live life the way you want to live it. What have you got to lose? You've tried it your way and haven't gotten the job you want. Now try it a different way.

As you read this book, envision yourself working in your pajamas and think of all the money you will save by no longer having to commute to work. Read the steps, listen to the tips, and use the tools suggested to land an online teaching job. Focus your energy on the outcome you want to have. Doing one thing each day to move you in the direction of teaching online will help you to feel more confident about achieving your goal. No matter what it looks like or feels like now, keep imagining what it will be like when you are educating online.

May you have tremendous success on the journey. Let's get started!

PART ONE
Fundamentals

Success is to be measured not so much by the position that one has reached in life as by the obstacles that he has overcome.
— Booker T. Washington

Success is a matter of understanding and religiously practicing specific, simple habits that always lead to success.
— Robert J. Ringer

What's Going On?

Education is the most powerful weapon which you can use to change the world. – Nelson Mandela

Education is that whole system of human training within and without the schoolhouse walls which molds and develops men. – W. E. B Du Bois

Education is an extremely important tool in navigating life's journey, but the process of education has changed from a formal, rigid classroom setting to a more open, flexible, and inclusive structure. Education today allows people to have access to a myriad of topics, using various modalities and teachers located all around the world, 24/7 and 365 days of the year.

Many questions have been raised about what is happening to the traditional system of higher education, why so many online schools are popping up, and why so many traditional schools now offer online programs. The emergence of such programs has created a great deal of uncertainty surrounding future employment opportunities. Some instructors state that they are afraid they won't be ready for future teaching opportunities or that online professors will take the jobs of those who teach in the traditional classroom. Many also express concern about not having the technological skills to compete in the workplace.

Various online adjunct groups and blogs continually debate whether on-site teaching opportunities are drying up and whether online teaching will be required in the next few years. Some common questions include:

- Why are many traditional nonprofit brick and mortar schools now offering online programs?

- What happened to the on ground teaching opportunities? Are they drying up?

- Is teaching online really going to be required in the next few years?

Many other people want to know what to do in order to prepare for the shift in the way instruction is delivered. They also want to know what is going on with existing and future teaching opportunities.

BACKGROUND

Major changes are taking place in the educational system. The reason is simple: leaders in education are responding to the market or what business people term the law of supply and demand. Researchers have conducted numerous studies to ensure that education is strategically positioned for the future. What some might not realize is that higher and continuing education is a business. Whether for profit or not, organizations must be administered in such a way that their mission and goals are achieved and comply with applicable rules, policies, and regulations. For many schools and businesses, online learning is part of a strategic plan to ensure that they remain viable and thriving entities.

Did you know that even government recognizes that online education makes great sense? Florida's legislature is now working on a law that will allow charter schools to exist online. Can you imagine a totally virtual charter school? A paradigm shift has begun, and it isn't going away. People want the opportunity and flexibility to learn in an online environment, and the jobs that make this possible - jobs for online administrators, developers, facilitators, teachers, professors, researchers, instructors, lecturers, authors, and contractors—are out there and will continue to increase. You just have to know where to look for them and what to do to get them.

Opportunities are plentiful. Don't limit yourself to virtual courses in higher education. Investigate a multitude of online teaching opportunities such as telecourse, webinars, high schools, curriculum developers, researchers, and trainers. With the technology available today, you don't need to wait on someone to hire you. Design your own courses and have others seek out your expertise. Keep your options open and be ready for all opportunities.

CHANGING TIMES

There has been a tremendous increase in the number of online students and programs. According to the November 2010 Sloan Report on Class Differences, "Over 5.6 million students were taking at least one online course during the fall 2009 term, an increase of nearly one million students from the previous year."

Onlineschools.org indicates that two-thirds of Americans spend approximately sixty-six hours per month on the computer, and this number does not include time spent on the computer at work. The statistics speak for themselves. Can you see why leaders in education are changing strategy to include people who want to be educated online? School administrators and business leaders must provide the courses, training, and products that consumers want and need in order to stay competitive.

Just in case you are not yet convinced, here are a few more mind-blowing statistics from the Sloan Report:

"Nearly thirty percent of higher education students now take at least one online course"; and "The twenty-one percent growth rate for online enrollments far exceeded the less than two percent growth of overall higher education student populations."

School administrators understand that in order to keep up with the demands of an ever-increasing online population, the number of new programs, courses, jobs, and teaching opportunities must increase. The economic downturn over the last few years has led to higher enrollment in both traditional and online courses; however, this demand has also pressured public and private institutions to offer additional online programs.

CHANGES IN DEMAND

Students, parents, educators, and administrators continue to look for improved educational opportunities. Consumers want courses, seminars, and training that allow not only traditional students aged 17-22 access but also older professionals, parents, and grandparents to achieve their educational aspirations. Customers want convenient, readily available courses, programs, seminars, and webinars they can take on their own time and this swelling demand has fueled change in the industry.

Business leaders have had to make educational options available without making people wait for the next on-campus offering. In the past students might have had to spend an extra semester in school or even derail their graduation plans if courses weren't offered when needed. Managers then began to realize that consumers had options. If one organization didn't have a desired course, another school or company would. Course flexibility and consumer expectations are a few more reasons why traditional schools now offer an abundance of online courses.

According to Mike Yoshimura, education is a 25 billion dollar industry and growing. What this means is that traditional campus teaching assignments will still be available since not all students desire to complete an entirely online program. Some people want and need face-to-face interaction with a teacher. However, both public and private nonprofit schools as well as businesses are adding online courses, so it makes sense if you plan on educating others your career that you get the skill set necessary to land all types of teaching assignments.

GLOBALIZATION

The nature of doing business has changed. We are now in a global economy where American companies and organizations are competing with their counterparts throughout the world. The Internet has allowed customers to have access to goods and services located anywhere. This paradigm shift has also occurred in education. Students can now participate in classes at institutions thousands of miles from their homes, 24/7 and 365 days of the year. As long as Internet connectivity is available, students can obtain degrees, training, certification, and the like without having to leave their residences.

Globalization opened up an entirely new market of customers, and organizations are stepping up to meet its needs. This development has led to an increase in the number of online schools, but traditional schools, corporations, and professional organizations are also now offering online learning. The advent of globalization is a win for students, a win for institutions, and a win for you because there is an abundance of jobs and opportunities for online teaching.

GOING GREEN

Rising gas prices have spurred the popularity of online education. Some administrators note that utilizing online learning decreases the carbon footprint of cars and mass transportation to and from campus. According to Simon Reichwald, around 79 percent of students live off campus, thousands of whom have decided to take courses online to save what they would otherwise spend on gas and travel. Online study diminishes vehicle emissions and makes use of computers, thereby mitigating harmful effects on the environment.

MODERN TECHNOLOGY

Information technology delivers education in a way that is creative, user-friendly, and effective. Courses can be taught 24/7 via modalities such as instant messaging, email, educational software, blogs, video conferencing, and streaming. Students can view presentations and videos, participate in teleconferences, and even download lectures they can listen to at their convenience.

Offering courses online soon became a smart business decision. The technology was already there; it just needed to be connected to the masses. Business leaders found that it didn't cost much to utilize the Internet for expanding their markets exponentially. Organizations offering online learning now had unlimited access to customers all over the world.

Researchers have also enumerated other benefits of allowing employees to work from home:

- Reductions in sick and personal days off

- Diminished turnover

- Increased retention

- Improved morale

- Increased productivity

- Decreased recruitment, training, and hiring costs

- Reduced parking costs

Allowing employees to work online, in short, is great for the corporate bottom line. Employees are happy, and business leaders save money.

Summary

1. A paradigm shift has occurred in teaching.
2. Online education is increasing.
3. Students demand online classes.
4. Online education makes good business sense.
5. Online teaching opportunities have increased and will continue to increase in the future.

Notes

_____

_____

_____

_____

_____

_____

Action Steps

_____

_____

_____

_____

_____

Who's Involved

Today knowledge has power. It controls access to opportunity and advancement. – Peter F. Drucker

Always walk through life as if you have something new to learn and you will. – Vernon Howard

Online education has evolved over the past decade. It began with the introduction of the Internet and was widely used for training and learning modules using web postings. What exists today is a tiered educational system that allows learners not only to take credit and non-credit courses but also to receive professional certifications and degrees including the Ph.D. Knowing who's involved and what online education entails is a great way to demonstrate your readiness to be an asset to a prospective employer.

History

The University of Phoenix was the first to launch an online university program in 1989, and Jones International University was the first to launch an entirely online accredited college in 1993. In the beginning online schools were for-profit organizations, but now, in order to keep up with demand and the changing climate of education, many nonprofits—public and private schools as well as professional organizations—offer some type of online courses or instruction. This development includes high schools, community colleges, and training organizations as well as Ivy League universities such as Harvard and Princeton.

STATISTICS

According to the National Center for Education Statistics, "Two-thirds of degree-granting postsecondary schools offer some form of online learning." Since courses are widely available, the jobs are out there. Kaplan University has over 35,000 online graduates, and the University of Maryland University College in 2011 had over 200,000 persons enrolled in online programs. Someone needs to teach all these students and develop courses. Why not you?

Online jobs are not limited to college and universities. There are now virtual high schools, charter schools, language schools, art schools, training organizations, and publishing firms in the market for online instructors.

SUBJECTS

A multitude of subjects are taught online. If you have the skills and experience, the opportunities are never-ending. Online education and training now include programs in these areas:

- Art
- Accounting
- Business
- Communications
- Computer Science
- Criminal Justice
- Curriculum Development
- English
- Foreign Languages

- General Equivalency Diploma (GED)

- Graphics Design

- High School

- Human Resources

- Information Technology

- Journalism

- Law

- Management

- Medical Billing

- Music

- Nursing

- Personal Development

- Paralegal

- Photography

- Self-Help

- Tutoring

- Web Design

- Writing

The above list is just a sample of online courses and opportunities. The roster of possibilities is endless depending on the expertise and experience you have.

As you review the options, don't forget that there are other ways to make money teaching online with organizations such as book publishers, educational software designers, curriculum developers, newspapers, magazines, and vocational schools. See job links in the appendix to gain access to websites, blogs, and resources you may never have thought about using. Open your mind to the abundant opportunities!

REPUTABLE OR NOT?

To verify an organization's professional reputation, you must know its operating status. Not all online schools are reputable or accredited. The federal Department of Education uses accreditation to ensure that schools operate at the highest standards for quality, professionalism, and ethics. To find out more information about accreditation, go to:

- **http://www.ope.ed.gov/accreditation**

If your goal is to teach at the primary or secondary level, accreditation is critically important because it will affect whether or not your experience or education is recognized by the organization for which you want to work.

In case you decide to stick with accredited online institutions, you can search the list at this site:

- **http://www.ope.ed.gov/accreditation/Search.aspx**

Perform a search for a specific school by its name, address, city, or state. Remember to keep your goals in mind while opening yourself up to the multitude of opportunities.

Just because a program or course is unaccredited, does not mean that it is not a viable venue for gaining valuable experience. Some professional organizations offer online career-related instruction or curriculum-development opportunities, and this is a great way to acquire experience with learning-management software.

PRIVATE SECTOR

Teaching online isn't just for primary, secondary, and higher education. It also includes many nonprofit and private businesses in the education arena. Here's a sample of some private organizations that have online jobs in such areas as translation, tutoring, and curriculum development:

- **https://careers-smarthinking.icims.com/jobs/intro**

- **http://www.tutorvista.com/teaching-jobs**

- **http://www.bilingualamerica.com/about/careers/**

- **http://www.tellmemore.com/about/aboutus/careers**

Even though these opportunities are not at accredited institutions, you can highlight this experience on your résumé to let prospective employers know that you are adept at working with learning-management systems and class facilitation.

MANY POSSIBILITIES

In one forum a potential instructor remarked, "I have been asked by XYZ school to submit my transcripts to continue the application process. Does anyone have any advice about this school?" To that inquiry another member of the forum replied, "Yes. Stay away. They have changed for the worse."

To this exchange I say, "Seize opportunities as they arise, but see what YOU think." Conduct some research on the Internet about the school and its history with students and employees. In most cases there will be many opinions, good and bad, but only YOU can decide what's best for you.

Millions of people are vying for online education positions. Keep your name in the forefront by gaining experience, which is one of the best ways to make an informed decision about what's in your own best interests.

THE CHOICE IS YOURS

I cannot advise you about whether or not to work for a school that is unaccredited, especially if you are new to online education and seeking the experience to propel you in the direction of your dream. Just know that experience can come from all types of educational opportunities. Know also that you can make money by teaching online for many reputable corporate entities as a facilitator or expert in a specific career area or trade.

Experience can be gained by educating online for a career school, training company or even a local library. The experience you gain is transferable to a multitude of situations. If your goal is to make money by teaching online, don't limit yourself. The possibilities are endless when you think beyond the box of teaching online for a postsecondary institution.

SUMMARY

1. Stay aware of the online-education players.
2. Online education is accredited and accepted.
3. There are a variety of online opportunities.
4. Don't limit yourself.

NOTES

_____

_____

_____

_____

_____

_____

ACTION STEPS

_____

_____

_____

_____

_____

Step I

Know What It Is

———— ✦ ————

An investment in knowledge pays the best interest.
— Benjamin Franklin

Knowledge has to be improved, challenged,
and increased constantly, or it vanishes.
— Peter Drucker

Many potential online instructors need help with understanding the various types of jobs, position requirements, and terms used in announcements. A common question asked by those seeking to teach online is:

- "What is the difference between a synchronous course and an asynchronous one?"

Knowing what online teaching entails is crucial to landing a job. Knowing the lingo helps you to sell your experience and skills to prospective employers. Knowledge of the terminology will also help you to communicate how you can be an asset to the organization in question. Before beginning to search for an online teaching job, however, you must know what to look for. Using the right terms and search words can make a huge difference in the number of hits you get when sorting through online opportunities and resources.

A few questions appear repeatedly in online discussions and blogs:

- Can you give me some idea of what to look for when searching for online jobs?

- What is an LMS?

- When I search for online jobs, should I use "e-teaching" or "e-learning"?

- If I search using "telecommuting," will it result in online education jobs?

Although answers to these questions vary depending on whom you ask, they usually concur. You have to know what online education is and what hiring officials look for in candidates' applications in order to be successful at landing an assignment. Below are some important tips for navigating the search process.

KNOW THE LANGUAGE

The first step is to know the basic words used to advertise online education jobs. Knowing the vernacular will help you to expand your search efforts and prepare you for the multitude of online positions and opportunities in education, teaching, development, and training.

Using this terminology in your search will assist you in getting the most comprehensive information. The following list includes the most common words, some of which are interchangeable, in online-education job announcements.

Adjunct. An instructor who does not hold a permanent position within an organization. Usually the assignment is contracted for a specified period of time. Therefore, there is no guarantee of future assignments.

Asynchronous Learning. Online learning that occurs while the instructor and students are not required to be in the course at any specific time. However, requirements must be filled by the instructor and students in terms of participation.

Computer-Based Training. Learning that occurs via the use of a computer but in many cases is self-paced.

Distance Learning/Education. Learning or education that takes place when the student and teacher are not physically located in the same space. This can be asynchronous or synchronous.

Distance Training. Education that occurs when the participant and instructor are not physically located in the same space. The term usually signifies instruction at the corporate or professional level.

E-Learning or E-Teaching. Education that takes place over a Local Area Network (LAN), Wide Area Network (WAN), or the Internet. It includes various types of computer-based learning.

Instructor-Led Training. Training led by the instructor at the same physical location over a LAN, WAN, or the Internet.

Learning Management System. Software program that allows for the administration, delivery, and tracking of classroom, online events, and/or e-learning programs. Common systems include Moodle, Blackboard, and eCollege.

Multimodal. Instruction that uses text, audio, and video.

Online Facilitation. Managing learners and the learning process through an online medium. Facilitators might not be required to have the same educational credentials as professors.

Online Learning. Electronic learning over the Internet.

Online Professor. Online postsecondary educator. Assignments can be full- or part-time, and the title will depend on degrees earned.

Online Teacher. Person who provides online schooling, education, and learning. This title normally is governed by state certifications or additional educational credits.

Online Training. Electronic learning over the Internet. It usually indicates professional or corporate instruction.

Synchronous. Online learning that takes place with an instructor and students at the same time. For example, the standard class meeting time is 6:00 pm EST, and everyone logs in during that time. Students have the ability to hear the instructor or post comments in real time.

Teleseminar. Live learning event with multiple attendees conducted over the telephone.

Telework. Job assignments not conducted in the traditional on-site office setting.

Virtual Learning Environment. Set of teaching and learning tools designed to enhance a student's learning experience by including computers and the Internet in the learning process.

Web-Based Training. Education or training delivered over a LAN, WAN, or the Internet. It can be computer-based, instructor-led, asynchronous, synchronous, or any combination thereof at the professional or corporate level.

Webinar. A seminar conducted over the Internet. It can be in real time or recorded for play-back at the participants' convenience.

Many of these terms may be used interchangeably in job announcements and descriptions. Know the lingo so that when you conduct an Internet search using any or all of the above terms, you get useful results. Knowing the terminology and incorporating it in your application package lets potential employers recognize your competence. Utilize the most widely used terms and definitions for the best results. Specific search strategies are discussed in Section Three.

SUMMARY
1. Know the language to improve search results.
2. Recognize the skills that hiring officials seek.
3. Understand the various modalities of online education.
4. Be familiar with the technology involved.

NOTES

_____

_____

_____

_____

_____

_____

ACTION STEPS

_____

_____

_____

_____

_____

_____

Step 2
Decide What Matters Most

Love what you do and do what you love. — Wayne Dyer

You are today where your thoughts have brought you; you will be tomorrow where your thoughts take you. — James Allen

Do you know why you want to teach online? Is it your desire to help others or have more flexible work hours? Will it give you more time to spend on personal interests and family or the ability to work while on travel? There are many benefits for online teachers, trainers and developers. Most that educate online cite that they enjoy having the flexibility to work but also have time during the day to focus on other interests. Yet one of the most widely requested answers still remain:

WHY TEACH ONLINE?

This answer can vary from individual to individual but here are some common reasons based on research, personal knowledge and experiences of those successfully teaching online. Only you can decide what factors make you want to be an online educator. Below are the most commonly cited benefits as well as drawbacks to online education.

Benefits

Access – as long as you have access to the internet and a computer you can instruct. One associate professor was called to active duty in Iraq, but was still able to conduct her courses through the use of her laptop and satellites. She not only fulfilled her obligations to the school but her willingness to teach on the battlefield allowed other soldiers and students to continue their studies. The instructor's battle field experiences were shared in the classroom instruction in support of the concepts in the textbooks. This gave students a real world view of the power of online learning even during times of war as well as drove home the point of business continuity planning.

Additional Source of Income – many work in the online education environment part time. It allows for instructors to supplement their income without having to incur additional expenses such as travel or hours away from home.

> One online curriculum developer remarked, "I love the income that I get from doing part time work. No matter whether I live in the U.S., Africa or Asia, I know the course pay will not decrease. The ability to use my teaching pay in a place where the cost of living is cheaper than in the US is definitely a bonus."

Autonomy – instructors can use much of their professional experiences and training in the course room. As long as the requirements are met, instructors often are encouraged to add additional relevant course materials such as real world case studies, videos, presentations, interviews, blogs, etc. One professional drummer that toured the world with Miles Davis instructs students through video mail, instructional DVDs, CDs and video conferencing. Some of the more requested online music instructors make more than six figures per year.

Connection to global community of instructors - since online employees regularly do not see their counterparts face to face, there are online blogs, groups and chats for educational faculty to share stories, tools, tips and mentor each other for online success.

> One instructor commented, "Our instructors try at least every other month to have local meet and greets for educational staff in similar geographical areas. It helps us to put faces with names and not feel so isolated. It also fosters camaraderie and sharing."

Convenience – most online education is asynchronous and available 24/7, so students and instructors pick the times that work best for their schedules.

> An instructor commented, "I can get an assignment with an Ivy League school without having to leave my home to fight rush hour traffic or relocate to another state. I can grade papers at midnight so that I don't take away from family time."

Continuous training and workshops – since learning in many instances takes place online and in most cases without the benefit of the instructors' voice or face, instructors must be well versed in providing tools and techniques that help students learn, keep them motivated and interested. This lends itself to administrators ensuring that instructors have software, tools and training to be successful. Online training in effective course development, blogging, presentations, communication and graphics are just a sample of the continuous training available to online educators.

> A facilitator commented, "I love that the company provides additional professional development courses and webinars monthly, to make sure our skills stay current, this is all at no cost to the staff."

Flexibility – since the course is not in a physical location, you can teach anywhere as long as there is an internet connection. In most cases you are not required to be online at specific times of the day. I've had the pleasure of teaching and working online while sitting on the beaches of Hawaii, Mexico and Jamaica, while on cruise ships and even in Africa. When I relocated from Washington DC to Florida, I never missed a beat. I was able to conduct my courses at various hotels, airports, libraries and coffee shops until I was settled in my new home with my high speed internet connection.

Free time for other endeavors – because most courses are asynchronous this allows instructors to work at times convenient for their schedules. If you work better at night then you can access your class at 10:00 pm after the family or other responsibilities are taken care of. Some online instructors comment that they love the freedom of being able to take the kids to school, pick them up and participate in all their children's activities or have the opportunity to work while the kids are asleep.

Hiring fairness - online educational opportunities are open to all regardless of race, color, gender, weight or physical agility, etc. As long as you have the education, skills and credentials, you are a candidate. During this economic downturn, many over the age of 55 have struggled to find work. According to the U.S. Department of Labor, unemployment for those over 55 has increased significantly. Working online is one way to fairly compete. Older workers have a great chance of being employed because many of them have years of education and practical experience that can be brought into the classroom.

My first online adjunct mentor had physical limitations and was confined to a wheelchair. He said,

> "Online instructing gave me access to jobs that I know would never be possible if I was required to travel every day to an on ground campus location. Online instructing allowed me to have a fulltime job with benefits, doing what I love without having to leave the house."

He felt that working online allowed him to bypass any perceived disadvantage or hiring bias because of his physical limitations.

Gain teaching experience – since there are a variety of online positions, you can use your education and professional experience as the platform to propel you into a teaching job. One online instructor commented,

> "I didn't have teaching experience but I had ten years of law enforcement/security experience, a high level security clearance and a Bachelors Degree. I always felt the desire to teach but thought I needed previous teaching experience. A friend told me about a private security firm that needed

online instructors, I applied and the rest is history. I've been teaching online for the past five years."

Interact with global students – because learning takes place online and in most cases 24/7 you have the opportunity to teach students located around the globe. This makes for diverse discussions and perspectives.

> An instructor stated, "One student was taking the international business course I taught from Egypt. It was astonishing to hear his accounts of the business environment in his country and some of the challenges faced for entrepreneurs. The entire class was able to hear a current, relevant global perspective from a peer. It was truly enlightening."

Jobs for Non Traditional workers – pregnant or working mothers, residents of remote areas or workers that need American Disability Act accommodations can all serve as online education facilitators. As long as they meet the minimum requirements and have access to the internet, they are just as viable a candidate as any other.

Learn new technology – leaders in the online education business know the competition is steep, so ensuring they provide students and staff with the most current and reliable software is critical. Many schools not only offer a sound platform for course delivery, but provide additional free technology and professional development courses so that instructors and students can maximize available technology resources such as social networking, blogging, video streaming, video conferencing as well as web development and branding.

> One instructor commented, "I've learned how to develop web pages, set up blogs and create video teleconferences all on the internet, free of cost by my employer. I feel equipped to handle any future technology requirements."

Marketable Skills – the global economy is heavily reliant on knowledge and technical skills. Having the experience of various software packages, facilitation methods and experience working with diverse groups can set you apart from others seeking the same positions.

An online adjunct professor stated, "I've been teaching online for over seven years. I have learned various educational software packages as well as productivity software. I have been able to use my expertise in blogging, social networking, presentations and course development to change my career path and earn a promotion."

Peer mentoring – since you don't have the benefit of face to face meetings, many schools assign peer mentors for first time instructors to ensure course facilitation success. Even many seasoned instructors have course leads to interact with and learn from.

> One online course developer commented, "Having a course mentor allowed me to learn company best practices and design requirements. This definitely cut down the learning curve."

Record of participant interaction – usage of online software records students' access and time spent in various course modules. This allows instructors immediate use of metrics and data to ascertain student learning and comprehension. If or when needed, proactive measures can be swiftly implemented for student learning issues or concerns.

> In the 2008 Educators in American Online Universities Study, one instructor commented, "I can see where students spend the majority of their time online. This helps me better prepare my interactions with students."

Stepping stone to full time online opportunities – some begin the journey with a part time online assignment with the hopes of becoming full time after serving a probationary period. Although many believe, there are no full time online education positions; that is not the case. You will see several in Part Two of the text.

> A full time online professor said, "I was at the right place at the right time. The announcement was posted internally for a full time entrepreneurship professor. Had I not taken the part time position and done a great job, I know I would

not have the full time opportunity since it was only open to current staff."

No Dress Code– when you work from home you can work in your pajamas and slippers. Since no one is there to see you, you have the luxury of being comfortable in what works best for you. Another benefit is that you save money on buying work clothes since they usually are not needed. One online facilitator commented,

> "I don't know how to fully express the happiness and satisfaction as well as the thousands of dollars I've saved from not having to buy work clothes over the past 5 years since working fulltime online. I love it!"

Drawbacks

Although there are many benefits that online educators capitalize on, there are also quite a few reported disadvantages. Online educating is not for everyone. A number of unfavorable factors are situational and can depend on the organization or institution where you instruct. These concerns in many cases are dependent upon the level and skill of the instructor. For some, there can be a large learning curve at the onset of the first course, training or assignment. As you become more proficient, hopefully the magnitude of these issues decrease.

A common question, I get asked:

- Is instructing online easier than traditional face to face teaching?

The answer to this question like many of those before is dependent upon the respondent as well as the organization.

Some Truth

People tend to think online teaching or training might be less work, however you must remember that most of the communication, grading and instruction must be word processed and posted in the computer for easy retrieval and complete by mandated due dates. So becoming technically savvy at least at the level of knowing how to use word processing software and productivity tools such as email, voice mail and instant messaging are crucial to online educating success. This same level of expertness might not be required for on ground courses since you have the availability of face to face lectures and communication. Below is a list of some common drawbacks expressed by online educators.

Additional duties not required of on ground staff – since in most cases of online teaching, students don't have the benefit of seeing the instructor and asking questions in real time, instructors might have to supplement personal interaction with other measures such as phone calls or chat sessions.

> An instructor commented, "I am required to phone all students during the first week of school. This takes up a great deal of my time and I have been fussed at a time or two by students who did not appreciate the phone calls."

Business minded, focused on the numbers – some online educators' state that because many of the online businesses are for profit, the main goal is to make money and meet sales numbers. If you don't have students, you don't make money. So this mindset could cause pressure for instructors to constantly be concerned about student retention and in some cases be the basis of teachers' fear of job loss which could lead to instructors posting inflated grades.

Employment at will – in many cases, especially online post secondary education there is no tenure/promotion or guarantee of future assignments. Assignments are made on a term by term basis and a new contract must be signed for each new course. This form of employment at will is very common especially for part time facilitators and adjunct instructors. However, this may not be the case for other organizations in online education such as book writers, course developers or subject matter expert positions. Yet many complain about the lack of security in online teaching.

Interruptions for non work issues – some online educators complain that getting interrupted with household chores remains a huge distraction. Cleaning, running errands or making service calls takes up time that should be used for working.

> One instructor stated, "Since I am at home, my spouse
> thinks I can do all the household chores. I must tell my
> family that even though I am home, I am working. I had to
> have a talk with my family to outline my work from home
> hours, to minimize the disruptions."

Isolation – online work is normally not conducted in a traditional office with others, as a result, working alone and the lack of regular interaction with students or peers might make some instructors lonely.

Lack of control – many online courses are configured to be instructor or facilitator transparent to allow for consistency and continuity, therefore in some cases changes to the look and feel of the course are prohibited. Also evaluation methods might be predesigned therefore the control to assign weights for assignments is not available.

Lack of compensation in relation to skill set or work hours – some feel that the pay for part time, adjunct or contract instructors lags in relation to on ground or face to face salaries.

> In a 2008 study conducted by Educators in American Online
> Universities, one respondent stated, "Pay is not representative
> of the skills brought to the table or the amount of time
> needed to facilitate the course and grade papers."

Many online educators state that more time is needed when initially starting but after you become seasoned; the time needed in most cases usually decreases because of your proficiency and efficiency.

Lack of training (dependent upon organization) – in many cases before you begin an online assignment, there will be some type of training or mentoring to prepare you for the organization's way of doing business, however the learning might be static and not varied based on the level of the learner. If you don't meet the course requirements in the specified timeframe or need additional time or assistance, you might have to retake the training or possibly not be offered the job.

Lack of recognition – since many postsecondary online positions are not offered tenure, promotion, research grants, research assistance, additional training or recognition for professional scholarship, some academic faculty in which academia is a career; do not deem these types of positions viable.

Lack of medical and health care – there are many part time or adjunct online educator positions and a great deal of organizations that have these types of positions do not provide health benefits for non full time employees.

Pay for performance issues – researchers have shown that increases in pay for part time online educators still lags behind their full time counterparts. Part time instructors might not receive funding for departmental or administrative duties like, professional development or travel such as those given to full time counterparts.

Readiness is variable - not everyone is suited for online learning as a result, instructors might have to deal with varying attitudes of online learners. Some students are ready and understand the commitment and organization skills needed to be successful, while there are others that think online education is easy, so they won't login the classroom frequently. When this happens, students might try to rush assignments at the last minute. This can put undue pressure on the educator to grade late or rushed projects that don't meet assignment criteria.

Stringent due dates – timely feedback is critical to the success of online education, therefore due dates for feedback and deliverables may be more aggressive than in the traditional classroom or on ground training and development settings.

Time consuming – due to the lack of personal interaction, additional communication and feedback must be given to ensure students comprehend the material.

> In the Educators in American Online Universities Study, one adjunct professor commented, "It is very time consuming, if you have 18 to 20 students, they have assignments sometimes 2 to 3 per week, if you have 18 to 20 students, times with 3 assignments per week, imagine, how much you are scoring.

There have been times I have been up all night grading assignments."

However a different instructor admitted,

"The time saved not having to travel and perform face to face lectures is worth the time being at home grading additional assignments."

Remember what is a negative circumstance or situation for one individual, might be a positive situation for another. It is up to you to decide what is a benefit or deterrent.

Varied student learning levels – since many online schools have open enrollment that is when basic minimum qualifications are met, students are enrolled in the curriculum. Facilitators may have to spend additional time teaching English, math and reading skills to those that are not versed in these subjects. Instructors could also be required to mentor participants to help them understand the individualized, active and goal oriented approach to online education and training.

According to one instructor in the Educators in American Online Universities study, "Many students enrolled in my class writing skills are not good, and then they can get very upset if they don't get 100% on everything."

Is This for Me?

After reading common positives and negatives of educating, it's time to take a short assessment to ascertain your willingness and readiness to delve into making money educating online. Remember you must make the decision that is best for your career or life. However you can use this checklist to help you make an informed decision.

Online educating might be for you if:

- You want to educate others but don't want to speak in front of students in a traditional classroom setting

- You don't mind not having face to face interaction with clients, colleagues and students

- You enjoy using technology such as instant messaging, blogging, email and video mail to communicate

- You don't mind students calling you at home or on your cell

- You enjoy using a word processor and providing students effective and in depth feedback on assignments

- You are willing to work with all types of students with different skill levels. Remember some schools and organizations have open door policies so student readiness and learning can vary.

- You are organized, great at time management and meeting online deliverables.

- You like getting participants actively involved in the learning process.

ONLINE INSTRUCTOR CHECKLIST

This list provides some of the common attributes that make great online educators. Take the assessment to determine if online educating is right for you. Place a check beside the level of your skills.

Organization Skills
- ✓ Excellent
- ✓ Good
- ✓ Okay
- ✓ None

Time Management Skills

- ✓ Excellent
- ✓ Good
- ✓ Okay
- ✓ None

Motivation to Succeed
- ✓ Excellent
- ✓ Good
- ✓ Okay
- ✓ None

Comfortable Learning New Technology
- ✓ Excellent
- ✓ Good
- ✓ Okay
- ✓ None

Ability to Work Unsupervised
- ✓ Excellent
- ✓ Good
- ✓ Okay
- ✓ None

Learning Management System Knowledge
- ✓ Excellent
- ✓ Good
- ✓ Okay
- ✓ None

Technological Proficiency
- ✓ Excellent
- ✓ Good
- ✓ Okay
- ✓ None

Access and usage of tools:
- ✓ Fax
- ✓ Modem
- ✓ Computer
- ✓ High Speed Internet
- ✓ Voice Mail
- ✓ Telephone

✓ Productivity Suite including word processing, presentation and spreadsheet software
✓ Web Camera
✓ Microphone
✓ Teaching methods such as blogs, video, teleconference, instant message and chat

If you checked excellent or good for the required skills and checked all the tools needed, online educating might be for you.

SUMMARY

1. Online education has plusses and minuses
2. What a benefit is for one person might be a drawback to another, so you decide.
3. Know the basic educator requirements
4. Understand the tools involved

NOTES

_____

_____

_____

_____

_____

_____

ACTION STEPS

_____

_____

_____

_____

_____

_____

PART TWO
Preparation

*Before everything else, getting ready is the secret to success. –
Henry Ford*

*Anticipate meeting obstacles but also anticipate overcoming
them. – Emmanuel Segui*

Step 3

Do Your Homework

———◆·❀·◆———

I hear and I forget. I see and I remember. I do and I understand. — Confucius

Be a lifelong student. The more you learn, the more you earn and the more self-confidence you will have. — Brian Tracy

If you've completed the assessment in the previous chapter and decided that online educating is right for you, you are well on your way, but before applying for online jobs read this section to get ready. Do the research to understand what it takes to develop an effective application packet. Preparation is crucial to setting yourself apart from the multitude of people aspiring to land an online teaching job. Thousands want to educate online, and you must ensure that when recruiters sift through piles of applications and résumés they stop at yours. So give them a reason. If you take the time to complete the simple steps outlined in this book, you can position yourself beyond the competition.

I've used these steps to secure my online jobs, and I coach others using the same steps I am presenting to you. With these few tools many have landed assignments in online education. They are now living their dreams of working outside an office and making money anywhere in the world. Remember to take the necessary time in preparing your application materials. Then let your qualifications speak for themselves to show that you are the best candidate for the position.

Before submitting a résumé, vita, or any other document in response to a position in online education, make sure you know what is required in terms of education, skills, work hours, duties, and software knowledge. You then can tailor your application materials to meet the needs of the organization. This alone will set you apart from other job candidates.

Use the Internet to find available positions. You will find that jobs are advertised not only on widely recognized sites such as monster.com and careerbuilder.com but also on those of professional organizations, governmental entities, schools, blogs, and online groups. Practice searching for openings in online education until you are comfortable with the process.

Remember too that not all opportunities will be posted online. Therefore, you need to know where to look to find positions advertised only within organizations. In Part Three of this book I discuss how to find opportunities not publicly listed.

Keep in mind that, when the right position is not available, you can always develop your own online courses, teleseminars, and webinars to sell to the online community or use as examples of your knowledge, skills, and abilities. Organizations such as Mindflash can help you to get the courses you develop sold online. For more information go to the following site:

- **http://www.mindflash.com/sell-courses-online/**

Stay Abreast of the Online Industry

Pay attention to new laws, regulations, schools, programs, and opportunities in the online industry. Know the terminology and use the Internet to sign up for automatic news alerts from higher-education sources such as these:

- ❖ Academic Careers – www.academiccareers.com

- ❖ Academic Keys – www.academickeys.com

- ❖ Academic Teaching Jobs – www.academploy.com

- ❖ Academic 360 – www.academic360.com

- ❖ Adjunct Nation – www.adjunctnation.com

- ❖ Adjunct World – www.adjunctworld.com

- ❖ Christian University Jobs – www.christianuniversityjobs.com

- ❖ Chronicle of Higher Education – www.chronicle.com

- ❖ Department of Education – www.ed.gov

- ❖ Higher Education Jobs – www.higheredjobs.com

- ❖ Higher Education Recruitment Consortium – www.hercjobs.org

- ❖ Higher Education Space – www.higheredspace.com

- ❖ Inside Higher Education – www.insidehighered.com

- ❖ Teacher Jobs – www.teacherjobshelp.com

- ❖ University Jobs – www.universityjobs.com

- ❖ Women in Higher Education – www.wihe.com

News feeds have valuable information on recruitment, hiring, and economic conditions in the industry. Conducting a simple Google search for online education laws will direct you to sites such as

- **elearners.com/guide/faq-glossary/education-laws/**

that detail regulations governing online education. Knowledge of the regulations will help you to demonstrate familiarity with the industry. This is one more thing to set you apart from the competition.

GET A JUMP ON THE COMPETITION

Be proactive while conducting your research for jobs in online education. Use the Internet to find a list of online schools and common positions. Dig deeper to identify specific Human Resource personnel, department chairs, recruiters, and hiring officials in the area in which you seek to instruct.

Contacting a specific person will set you apart from those who submit generic applications.

Conducting a simple Google search for "online schools" will guide you to sites such as these:

- **http://www.accredited-online-colleges.com**

- **http://www.onlinehighschool.org**

- **http://www.accreditedonlineschools.org**

- **http://www.allonlineschools.com**

- **http://www.directoryofschools.com**

- **http://www.elearners.com/colleges**

- **http://www.guidetoonlineschools.com**

These sites contain detailed lists of accredited online schools. The lists will help you to uncover the actual hiring or departmental staff information needed to send unsolicited applications to colleges and universities. There is also an extensive list of schools with online classes located in the appendix. Go above and beyond the online application, following up with a phone call or email to the contact persons. Let them know that you are interested in a position. Send résumés and ask questions to gain more insight into their hiring practices. Don't forget that many career schools, professional, and for-profit educational organizations will have online positions too.

According to the director of learning at a well-known community college, "It might hurt you to wait until an actual job announcement is posted because then everyone has seen the job and hundreds, if not thousands, normally apply." Don't wait until a job is posted. Be one of the first to get your application materials to the right hiring official. Get a jump on the competition by being proactive.

Job Requirements

Before you submit an application, you should know the common requirements for positions as an online educator. You can do a Google search for "Online Professor," "Online Teacher," or "Online Instructor" to get this basic information. More details on how to conduct an in-depth job search are provided in Part Three of this book.

Keep in mind that each opportunity can vary regarding minimum qualifications. Do you have the education needed? Do you have the minimum skills needed? By reviewing online job announcements you will get an understanding of the experience, skills, and education needed to land a job. You also can determine whether there are some areas in which you need more training.

Some positions require a Ph.D. with research skills, while others want instructors with practical work experience. Some religiously affiliated organizations might require faith statements, while others might call for a specialty certificate or license. There are vacancies for all levels of online educators within such institutions as community colleges, four-year universities, companies, publishers, management organizations, and education-related businesses. Be open to all types of online possibilities to get access to an abundance of opportunities.

AVAILABLE POSITIONS

Listed below are some diverse but representative job descriptions taken from the Internet.

> **Position** – Full-Time Business Faculty, For-Profit Online University
>
> **Education** – Ph.D. or D.B.A. in a related field from a regionally accredited college or university
>
> **Experience** – Potential faculty should have at least five years teaching experience and at least five years related work experience. Experience in simulation-based teaching, especially asynchronous simulation-based teaching, and/or experience with other experientially-based, innovative teaching techniques highly desirable.
>
> **Skills** – Must have outstanding written communication skills, excellent motivational and instructional skills, and ability to facilitate diverse groups.

Position – Adjunct Education Faculty, Early Childhood, Non-Profit University

Education – Master's degree in Early Childhood education or closely related field and a minimum of 24 graduate hours in Early Childhood education

Experience – Experience in online teaching required. Must be willing to use and develop courses using the online learning platform, engage in rigorous curriculum review, and participate in professional development activities sponsored by the University.

Position – Full-Time Training and Instruction Manager, Non-Profit University

Education – No minimum specified

Experience – Two years teaching experience, preferably in high-need schools or with high-need populations. Track record of raising student achievement.

Position – Full-Time Criminal Justice Instructor, Non-Profit University

Education – Master's degree required. Must have minimum of 18 graduate hours in Accounting. M.B.A. preferred.

Experience – Ability to work effectively with supervisors, colleagues, staff, and students as part of an education team. Write and update curricula including course outlines and syllabi as required by the institution or industry trends. Teaching experience preferred. Must demonstrate ability to develop and teach courses online.

Skills – Blackboard Vista 8, Google Apps, Adobe Presenter, Camtasia, SnagIt, Jing, and SoftChalk. Web 2.0 tools such as Audacity, Prezi, and BigBlueButton are being considered.

Position – Contract Trainer, Non-Profit University

Education – No minimum specified

Experience – Must have a proven ability to communicate effectively both in writing and verbally with management and peers on issues, risks, opportunities, and general progress toward business goals. Ability to use appropriate skills in the areas of project coordination, multitasking, prioritization of demands, group discussion, training, facilitation, decision-making, communication, and time management.

Skills – Multilingual candidates are always a positive asset. Successful candidates must be skilled communicators comfortable in dealing with diverse clients in unique and often novel situations, with a strong focus on value to the customer.

Position – Adjunct Faculty, Multiple Disciplines, Non-Profit Christian University

Education – Master's degree, including a minimum of 18 hours in the teaching area

Experience – Superior interpersonal, customer-service, presentation, and communication skills required. Creative, innovative, and problem-solving skills also required. Proven organizational skills and ability to complete assignments in timely fashion and accurately with minimal supervision.

Skills – Demonstrated strengths in teaching at the college level are essential. Proficiency in MS Office, Blackboard, and the Internet.

*Must apply using the University's automated system.

Position – Adjunct Faculty, Multiple Disciplines, Online University

Education – Master's degree including a minimum of 18 hours in the teaching area. Prefer Ph.D. or equivalent in desired teaching areas.

Experience – Prior college-level teaching experience with the adult and or military student population is preferred and highly valued. Experience with case-based assignments and teaching in online higher education preferred. Excellent written communication skills.

Skills – Ability to engage students effectively in written communication. Student support and academic coaching that yields performance improvement.

Position – Adjunct Faculty, Nursing, Non-Profit University

Education – Doctorate in Nursing (D.N.P. or Ph.D.) or closely related field. Family Nurse Practioner certification strongly preferred.

Experience – Must have professional and at least one year college teaching experience, preferably online, with a focus in related areas.

Skills – Research with published articles on course topic in peer-reviewed journals is preferred. Successful candidates must reside in the United States. Broadband Internet access required.

Position – Virtual High School Teacher (Full- or Part-Time), Online High School

Education – Minimum of a master's degree for undergraduate programs and a doctoral degree for graduate programs (unless waived by the College Vice President for Academic Affairs).

Experience – Prior teaching experience for grades 9-12.

Skills – Valid teaching certificate for the specific state.

Position – Academic Program Chair, Education Online, For-Profit University

Education – Not specified

Experience – Expertise in the subject matter of assigned courses/programs

Skills – Must be capable of providing leadership and inspiration to assigned faculty. Must be highly structured and organized. Must be sufficiently technically oriented to understand the technical objectives of assigned programs. Must be capable of writing in clear manner and delivering organized, informative presentations.

Position – Part-Time Content Writer, For-Profit Business

Education – Master's in English from a regionally accredited college or university

Experience – Writing educational content for courses, blogs, and websites

Position – Telecommuting LSAT Instructor, For-Profit Business

Education – Bachelor's or higher, J.D. preferred, 90th percentile or higher on LSAT

Experience – Previous training and experience are preferred.

Skills – MS Office and Outlook skills

Position – Academic Center Tutor, Mathematics, For-Profit Business

Education – Master's in math or statistics

Experience – Previous tutoring experience helpful. At least three years of teaching.

Skills – Ability to work with all levels of learners.

Position – Full-Time Educational Writer/Researcher, For-Profit Publisher
Education – None specified
Experience – Good at self-management and research, excellent English grammar and writing persuasively for educational, step-by-step tutorials that people can easily follow.
Skills – Strong desire to improve writing skills continuously.

Position – Certified Teacher, Music, Non-Profit School

Education – Minimum of a college degree from an accredited university
Experience – Highly qualified and certified to teach Music (K-12) in Virginia (appropriate to grade level and subject responsibilities).
Skills – Strong technology skills (especially with Microsoft OS and MS Office). Excellent communication skills, both oral and written.

As you can see, the requirements and qualifications vary for each position, but there are jobs out there if you know what to look for and how to apply. After reviewing the above online job descriptions, you can decide which types of positions work best given your education, skills, and goals.

COMMONLY USED TECHNOLOGY APPLICATIONS

Being tech-savvy and knowledgeable about commonly used applications will help position you above other applicants. Most job announcements require certain technical skills. If you are not comfortable with the following tools for online teaching, I suggest that you begin mastering them.

- **Blog** – Web site on which an individual or group of users record opinions, information, videos, and graphics on a regular basis. A blog can be used by educators to provide additional information to facilitate student learning. You also can create a blog to provide professional expertise on relevant topics.

- **Learning Management Systems (LMS)** – Software application for the administration, documentation, tracking, and reporting of online events, learning programs, and training content. Common software includes:

  - ❖ **Pearson eCollege**
  - ❖ **Blackboard (ANGEL, WEbCT)**
  - ❖ **Desire 2Learn**
  - ❖ **Moodle**
  - ❖ **Brainhoney**
  - ❖ **Sakai**
  - ❖ **WebTyco**

- **Microsoft Office** – Computer software program used to create, edit, and print documents, databases, spreadsheets, web pages, and visual presentations. It is available for both PC and MAC platforms.

- **Podcast** – Series of digital media files (audio or video) that are released at regular intervals and often downloaded.

- **Screencast** – Digital recording of computer-screen output, also known as a video-screen capture, that often contains audio narration software such as Jing and Screenr. It is free and used regularly.

- **Streaming** – Information/data delivered from a server to a host in real time. It can be video, audio, graphics, slide shows, web tours, or a combination thereof. Streaming also can be either a synchronous or an asynchronous broadcast. Blackboard purchased the two most common platforms, Elluminate and Wimba, to create Blackboard Collaborate.

- **Wiki** – Software that allows the creation and editing of web pages by various contributors using a web browser and simple mark-up language. A common wiki is Wikipedia, which is not used as an academic reference because the information may not be accurate, credible, or verifiable.

Online recruiters look for people who are comfortable with technology and can demonstrate such proficiency in their résumés, so you must know the most common software and tools used. Jobs as an online instructor require you to manage your time wisely and be very organized, since most likely you will establish your own schedule and work hours using technology. Organizational tools such as Google Calendar, Personal Digital Assistant, or eFax can also be listed on a résumé to let recruiters know you are adept at using technology. If there is some type of assessment before you are hired, more than likely your ability to use technology will be part of it. Therefore, the sooner you learn and master technology, the better. Evaluate your skill set, determine your weak areas, and do the work to land the job!

Summary

1. Stay abreast of online education to demonstrate knowledge.
2. Know the requirements for the job.
3. Obtain the essential skills or abilities.
4. Get experience with common educational tools, hardware, and software. Doing so will make you more marketable.

Notes

_____
_____
_____

Action Steps

_____
_____
_____

Step 4
Develop a Winning Application

Great things are not done by impulse but by a series of small things brought together. – Vincent Van Gogh

I can't change the direction of the wind, but I can adjust my sails to always reach my destination. – Jimmy Dean

Before you begin assembling an application package, you need to know what recruiters and hiring staff look for in a résumé. In many cases résumés are put through an electronic database to sort out applicants who demonstrate the knowledge, skills, and abilities that most closely match what is needed by the organization. Employers want to know that what you bring to the table aligns with the position and the organization's mission and goals.

When online positions are posted externally, hundreds start applying. Let me offer a brief but dramatic example. An instructor posted a position for an adjunct business instructor on one of the user groups in which I participate so that members would get the first shot at the job. The announcement was put on a major online job site the next day, and within two days it was removed because over 500 people had applied for the opening. What is a human resource professional to do? If you were the person reviewing 500 résumés, what would be your screening process?

Human Resource professionals have to quickly weed out applications that don't fit job requirements, spending time on the most promising ones. The situation I have described is common for positions in online education.

You've read the benefits of teaching online, and for many the positives outweigh the negatives including the hundreds who submitted résumés for that single job opening. In order to get your application placed at the top of the pile, let's start by learning what screeners look for in an application packet.

Application Package

The application packet should demonstrate your ability to be an asset to the organization in question. The items contained in it should be clear, succinct, and relevant in relating your qualifications to what is sought in the job description. There are several items you should have readily available before applying.

- ❖ General Cover Letter – Introduction to you and your abilities. The boilerplate letter can be tailored to address the specifications for each job.

- ❖ Résumé or Vita – Summary of your education, skills, and experience in relation to a finely tuned objective.

- ❖ Statement of Teaching Philosophy – This document details your teaching approach, methods, and expertise.

- ❖ Statement of Faith (if applying to religion-based institutions) – Narrative of religious beliefs and affiliations as well as how they will be utilized in achieving position goals.

- ❖ Three to Five References – People with knowledge of your education, skills, or abilities. The list should include an address, phone number, and email for each person.

- ❖ Three Letters of Recommendation – Detailed written accounts of your education, knowledge, skills, and abilities, preferably written within the last three years.

❖ Unofficial Transcripts – Student record of all courses taken. Normally official and sealed transcripts from each school attended are required by hiring officials before you are accepted on staff.

❖ Student, Faculty, or Professional Evaluations – Documents or statements that demonstrate your expertise, skills, and job effectiveness.

When you apply for online positions, speed is critical. Responding quickly demonstrates that you are accessible, organized, and reliable. Have the above materials ready in PDF format to distribute when needed.

HUMAN RESOURCE SCREENING

Human Resource managers, as already noted, have to sift through hundreds of applications for jobs in online education. To do this in the most efficient way possible, they use electronic systems to review résumés for the skills, knowledge, and education that best fit the position. Business owners have to do more with less, so the goal is to use technology to fill jobs faster while using fewer people hours. When your résumé is scanned electronically, the computer software will pick up on key words.

Without the right words your résumé could be overlooked or rejected. The language that should be included in your résumé is detailed in the job posting. Make sure that you closely review the terms used in each job listing. If you can honestly attest that you have performed the tasks and have the necessary education or skills outlined in the job announcement, include them in your application materials. Below are some résumé-scanning systems commonly used by hiring personnel.

1. Résumé Management System is a desktop application system that was developed to assist recruiters in managing résumés. It is a fully automated system for reading, analyzing, sorting, storing, tracking, and segregating such documents.

2. Resumix is a system used by government agencies. This software replaces the manual review of applications with technology that matches qualified applicants with vacancies. The system

uses optical character recognition, imaging technology, and a patented skill-extraction system to "read" your résumé.

3. iCIMS software identifies the best candidates by providing applicant collection, parsing, and streamlining. Users can get detailed reports of those with key skills and required education. The information is stored in a database for easy retrieval and manipulation.

Hiring staff no longer have the time or resources to read hundreds of résumés. The process is now automated so that employers can easily identify the candidates whose qualifications best match a position. To get your résumé noticed by hiring personnel, learn how to incorporate essential terminology.

Résumé Essentials

There are some basic elements that each recruiter is searching for in a résumé. Before you submit your qualifications for consideration, be sure to complete the following steps.

Write a winning résumé objective or qualification summary. Reveal your professional goals but state them in a way that clearly communicates your interest in working for the targeted employer. Highlight the skills and education you bring to the table and illustrate how you can aid the organization in achieving its mission and goals. The résumé statement of objective or summary of qualifications should answer three questions:

- What type of work do you want?

- What are your main skills?

- How will you be an asset to the company that hires you?

Focus on how you can benefit the employer rather than on how the employer can benefit you. Conduct research so that you know the organization's mission and goals; then align your skills to correspond with them. Demonstrate how you will utilize technology and transferable skills like oral and written communication to enhance the position.

Example of Résumé Objective

Objective: To obtain a position as an online business instructor and utilize over ten years of practioner experience and five years of experience with online learning management systems, development, and facilitation to create interesting and educational courses that increase student learning.

Let's break down the above example.

- "Obtain a position as an online business instructor." This tells the reader what type of job you want.

- "Who will utilize over ten years of practioner experience and five years of experience with online learning management systems, development, and facilitation." This tells the reader what relevant skills and experience you bring to the table. It also indicates that you not only can you teach a course but also develop it and provide curriculum if necessary.

- "Create interesting and educational courses that increase student learning." This tells the reader that you are aware of the company mission and want to be on board to help achieve it.

Highlight sought-after skills by including key résumé terms. Developing an effective résumé is critical to landing the online job you seek. Position descriptions or vacancy announcements contain the terms hiring officials want to see in a résumé. Since many online jobs have the same basic requirements, here is a list of words that should be included in the education, skills, or job sections of your résumé to get it noticed not only by hiring staff but also by screening systems.

> **A:** Accomplished, achieved, acquired, adapted, addressed, adept, adjunct, administered, advised, allocated, analyzed, Angel, animated, answered, applet, applied, appointed, appraised, approved, arbitrated, assembled, assessed, assigned, assumed, assured, asynchronous, audited, authored, authoring, awarded

B: Balanced, Blackboard, blog, briefed, broadband, broadcast, broadened, browser, budgeted, built

C: Calculated, carried out, certificate, certification, certified, chaired, changed, chat, chatroom, coached, collaborated, communicated, compiled, completed, composed, comprehension, computed, computer, computerized, conceived, conceptualized, conducted, consolidated, constructed, consulted, Content Management System, contributed, converted, coordinated, corrected, counseled, course, courseware, created, creative, cultivated, curriculum, customer service, cyberspace

D: Database, decreased, defined, degreed, delivered, demonstrated, designed, Desire to Learn, determined, developed, devised, diagnosed, digital, directed, discovered, distance, distributed, diverse, documented, doubled, drafted, DSL (Digital Subscriber Line)

E: Earned, eCollege, edited, educated, effected, effective, electronic, eLearning, eliminated, email, empowered, engineered, enhanced, enlarged, ensured, established, estimated, eTeaching, evaluated, examined, exceeded, executed, expanded, explained, experienced, expert, explored

F: F2F (Face-to-Face), facilitated, faxed, filled, focused, forecast, formalized, formulated, found, founded, fulfilled, functioned, FTP (File Transfer Protocol)

G: Gathered, generated, globalization, Google, graded, granted, GUI (Graphical User Interface), guided, guest-lectured

H: Handled, headed, helped, high-speed, hosted, HTML (Hyper Text Mark-up Language)

I: Identified, ILS (Instructor-Led Training), implemented, improved, IMS (Instructional Management System), increased, influenced, initiated, innovated, innovative, inspected, installed, instant messaging, instituted, instruct, instructed, insured, integrated, interpreted, instructional, Internet, introduced, invented, investigated, ISP (Internet Service Provider), issued

J: Java, joined, justified, Jing

K: Kept, KMS (Knowledge Management System)

L: Launched, LCMS (Learning Content Management System), learned, learning, Learning Management System, lectured, led, licensed, link

M: Maintained, managed, mark-up, mastered, measured, mediated, met, modified, monitored, Moodle, motivated, motivational, moved, MP3, multicasting, multimedia, multilingual

N: Named, navigated, negotiated, nesting, net, netiquette, network, networked, newsgroup

O: Obtained, offline, online, opened, open source, operated, ordered, organized, overhauled, oversaw

P: Participated, patented, PDF (Portable Document Format), perceived, performed, persuaded, pixel, placed, planned, plug-and-play, podcast, posted, portal, prepared, presented, presentation, presided, processed, procured, produced, productivity, professor, proficient, programmed, projected, promoted, proposed, provided, protocol, published, purchased, pursued

Q: Qualified, quality, quantified

R: Raised, ranked, rated, received, recognized, recommended, reconciled, recorded, recruited, redesigned, reduced, referred, reorganized, repaired, replaced, replied, reported, represented, researched, resolved, responded, restored, retention, revamped, reviewed, revised, role-play

S: Saved, scanner, scheduled, screened, Screencast, screen reader, screen shot, script, search engine, selected, served, serviced, shaped, shared, showed, simplified, skilled, solved, sorted, sought, spam, sparked, spoke, spreadsheet, staffed, started, steered, story board, stream, streamlined, strengthened, stressed, stretched, structured, student, studied, submitted, substituted, succeeded, suggested, summarized, superseded, supervised, supplied, surveyed, synchronous, systematized

T: Tackled, targeted, taught, teach, technology, telecommute, teleconference, teleseminar, telnet, tested, tracked, trained, training, transcribed, transferred, transformed, translated, transported, traveled, treated, trimmed, tripled, turned, tutored, tutorial

U: Uncovered, understood, understudied, unified, unraveled, updated, upgraded, upload, URL, utilized

V: Video, video conference, virtual, VLE (Virtual Learning Environment), verbalized, verified, virus, visited, VPN (Virtual Private Network)

W: Waged, WBT (Web-Based Training), web, webcast, WebCT, webinar, webpage, website, WebTyco, wiki, Wimba, weighed, wiki, won, worked, write, wrote, WWW (World Wide Web)

Y: Youtube

Specifically detail your expertise with the technology outlined in the job announcement. Since you are seeking a job as an online educator, demonstrating your adeptness in navigating the Internet and using common instructional technology is imperative. If you have any experience with the software applications and systems noted earlier, make sure you list them and provide specific examples with dates. You should conduct additional research to find out which systems are used at each organization and highlight those skills if you have them. Below is an example of relevant skills sought in a job announcement and the corresponding résumé detail:

Relevant Skills Sought in Job Announcement: Expert in the use of BlackBoard and eCollege educational systems for course facilitation.

Experience Detailed in Résumé: Used Blackboard to facilitate undergraduate business communications courses from 2006–present and eCollege to facilitate graduate entrepreneurship courses from 2008–present.

If you don't have the skills stipulated in a vacancy posting, you can easily obtain them. However, only put in your résumé what is true and can be proven because nearly all candidates will have to demonstrate those abilities during the interview process.

Include your professional online URLs. Before a candidate is considered, hiring officials usually conduct an Internet search for his or her professional, social, and community involvement. Do the work for them by including any URLs for your professional media, websites, and blogs such as LinkedIn, Facebook, or Myspace. I always include www.drcarolynedwards.com and the howtoteachonlinebook.com that highlight my expertise, experience, and publications. However, never list any personal sites! Indicate only those sites that document your ability to meet the job requirements and use technology successfully.

Develop a winning cover letter or email. Due to globalization in the business environment, the ways of submitting job applications have evolved. Sometimes you will send a cover letter, but for other positions you might send what I call a cover email. You can use the same body text for both. However, the headings for a letter versus an email will vary. Make sure that your wording in both, addresses the skills, education, and experience outlined in the position announcement.

The first paragraph in the cover document should always explain why you are writing. Get to the point and make it simple and plain. If you don't capture the reader's attention in the first two sentences, the rest of your document might never be read.

The next few paragraphs should clarify why the company ought to hire you. The most important information to include is how you will be an asset to the company by utilizing your knowledge, skills, and experience to help the organization achieve its goals. This can only be done if you know what its mission and objectives are.

In your last paragraph thank the recipient for his or her consideration and include your name, address, email, and telephone number. See this book's appendix for examples of a cover letter and cover email.

CREATE AN EFFECTIVE LIST OF REFERENCES

Choose at least three to five people who can vouch for your professional education, skills, abilities, or knowledge. Contact each person to inquire whether he or she would be comfortable with providing a reference. If the person agrees, add him or her to your list.

The name, title, address, telephone number, and email address of each reference should appear on the document. I suggest including professors, managers, course developers, supervisors, or colleagues who can attest to your proficiency. If you are applying to faith-based organizations, you should also include someone familiar with your religious beliefs and affiliations.

Example:

Name: Dr. Carolyn Edwards
Title: CEO, EdWorks
Address: PO Box 570555, Cutler Bay FL 33257
Phone: 786-309-1773
Email: dre@drcarolynedwards.com

DEVELOP A MUCH SOUGHT AFTER STATEMENT OF TEACHING PHILOSOPHY

Your formulation of a teaching philosophy does not have to be very lengthy. It is a general statement about your objectives, how you plan to achieve them, and why you wish to teach. These major components are detailed below.

1. What are your objectives, and what do you want to accomplish? After you have a clear understanding of what you want to accomplish, this information should align with the organization's

mission and goals. Keep hiring officials' attention by making your objectives congruent with the organization's needs.

2. Describe the method by which you will achieve the objectives. Be specific about methods you will use such as learning management systems, videos, webinars, blogs, and teleseminars to devise outcome-based learning environments. Highlight the technological skills, knowledge, and expertise you will use to achieve the objectives. Sell yourself and your abilities. Mention any courses, training, or textbooks that you've developed or published.

3. Articulate, lastly, why you want to engage in teaching. Tell the readers what is in it for them. For example, you can discuss the joy you find in online education by helping others to meet their educational needs.

I won't list a lot of teaching philosophies because you should develop your own based on your education, knowledge, and skills as well as what you wish to accomplish. Ohio State University's Center for the Advancement of Teaching provides several examples of teaching philosophies at this site:

- **http://ucat.osu.edu/portfolio/philosophy/Philosophy. html**

Just remember to follow the above steps and include the information sought by hiring officials.

SUPPLEMENTAL CREDENTIALS

After learning that a company is interested in your application, you might be required to submit additional materials such as written letters of reference, student or supervisory evaluations, and a statement of religious faith. Letters of references should document your actual knowledge, skills, and abilities for the positions you seek. The letters should be current (i.e., written within the last three years) and contain their authors' mailing address, telephone number, and email address.

If you are seeking a position with a religiously affiliated organization, prepare your statement of faith ahead of time so that, when asked for, you can submit the document expeditiously. Make sure that your statement details your values as well as how they fit in with the mission, vision, and goals of the organization in question. That, of course, will entail your doing some background research on the school or organization.

Get Feedback from Someone in the Field

Ask for a review of your application package by someone who is an online educator, hiring official, or career coach. Can't think of anyone? Draw on colleagues, online group participants, professors, and trainers. Communicating your needs will get you useful feedback from a qualified source. Check out theteachonlinebook.com, or you can always sign up for coaching at www.drcarolynedwards.com.

Here's a word of caution. There is no lack of people who will give an opinion, but your goal is to get responses from people who want to help you achieve your goal of teaching online. Filter the feedback; apply constructive advice to achieve your goals.

Summary

1. Keep your application information up to date.
2. Tailor your application materials for the actual job posting or position.
3. Include key terminology in your application materials.
4. Before submitting the application, make sure you have included all required documents and information.

Notes

_____
_____
_____

Action Steps

_____
_____
_____

Step 5

Look in the Right Places

—————◆◆◆◆◆—————

Ask and it will be given to you; seek and you will find; knock and the door will be opened to you. — Matthew 7:7

Success leaves clues. — Anthony Robbins

There are so many places to find online teaching jobs that applying for such positions can turn into a full-time endeavor. You can begin by looking at the list of schools with online programs in the appendix. Visiting each website and investigating not only the job openings but also specific departments and programs will keep you busy. If there is not a job listed for which you want to apply, begin gathering the names of major players such as department chairs, deans, Human Resource managers, etc. These are the people you will write to when you request information or submit your unsolicited application packet.

Hiring officials use a variety of online sites to post job openings. A representative for Northampton Community College commented, "Jobs are posted on the college website, national academic sites such as insidehighered.com, alumni organizations, local newspapers, and online learning networks. Jobs could also be posted in specific departments." The jobs are out there, so be proactive and don't limit your search options. Use all the resources available to you to find online teaching jobs.

Internet

Managers know the internet is a fast, inexpensive and convenient way to display job information and make it readily available to the masses. So use it to find leads by Googling careerbuilder.com and monster.com using such search terms as the following:

- adjunct online jobs

- k-12 online schools

- distance learning

- online adjunct

- online education jobs

- online instructor

- online professor employment

- online teacher

- online tutor employment

- telecommute teacher jobs

Write down your search words or bookmark them for easy retrieval in the future.

Online Job Sites

The following sites specifically list academic positions:

- www.academiccareers.com

- www.adjunctnation.com

- www.chronicle.com

- www.facultyfinder.com

- www higheredjobs.com

- www insidehighered.com/career

- www onlineadjunctjobs.net

- www scholarlyhires.com

- www tedjob.com

These sites focus on academic teaching positions; however, you also will be able to search for online administrative positions such as those of department chairs, deans, advisors, and registrars. Some sites allow you to set up a job-search profile to receive automatic emails regarding new positions. I suggest you do this so that relevant job announcements come directly to you.

SPECIFIC SCHOOLS AND ORGANIZATIONS

If you have already started to search for online teaching jobs, you may have noticed that not all schools with online programs have job postings on major academic sites. Some schools and organizations list jobs only on their main website. If you don't see a specific job listed, find an email address or contact number for the appropriate hiring official and send a request for information along with your résumé. You can even make a phone call to inquire about the application process.

Organizations may hire through a specific department that has an opening versus hiring through the central Human Resource office. Being proactive and not waiting for an actual job opening could actually make those with hiring authority remember your name and application materials. Use the list of schools with online programs in the appendix to locate organizations' web sites where you can search for job openings in your areas on interest. You then can make your appeal to the specific person who has the authority to hire.

By this stage of the book you should have your application materials ready. All you need to do now is to tailor your cover letter or introductory email and résumé statement of objective to demonstrate you can be an asset to the organization. Do the research, take action, and apply!

Alumni Organizations

You might be able to find jobs at your former educational institutions. Hiring officials sometimes post openings via their school's alumni group, thereby saving the cost of external advertising. Hiring former students also benefits officials because they know that alumni candidates are familiar with the school's curriculum, have fulfilled the mandatory academic requirements, and have their transcripts already on file. Former students benefit because they get access to job openings before they are announced to the general public.

Hiring officials in other organizations also allow former employees to have first access to current openings. As an added benefit many organizations offer former employees resources such as résumé preparation, counseling, job fairs, employment presentations, and even automatic job announcements through email. Take advantage of opportunities related to former associations. You just might land a job because of such connections.

Professional Organizations

What is your career concentration or specialty? Are you an IT professional? Business and management specialist? Nurse, electrician, or certified teacher? There are specialized organizations for almost every career specialty, and these organizations are great places to network and find out about online jobs. For example, professions such as teaching, healthcare, law, and business all have organizations dedicated to helping their members succeed. Many of these groups have yearly conferences where you not only can keep abreast of your specific specialization but also learn best practices in your field. You might even get a chance to attend a job fair at a professional conference where employers are looking for candidates with your experience and skill set. Here's a short list of career-specific organizations to get your started.

> **Academy of Health** – www.academyhealth.org
> **Academy of Management** – www.aomonline.org
> **American Association of Information Technology Professionals** – www.aitp.com

American Association of University Professors – www.aaup.org

American Bar Association – www.americanbar.org

American Educational Finance Association – www.aefa.cc

American Institute of Certified Public Accountants – aicpa.org

American Nurses Association – www.nursingworld.org

Association on Budgeting and Financial Management – www.abfm.org

Council of Supply Chain Management Association – cscmp.org

National Council of Teachers of English – www.ncte.org

National Education Association – www.nea.org

National Electrical Contractors Association – www.necanet.org

National Tax Association – www.ntanet.org

If your career specialty is not represented in the above list, conduct an Internet search for professional organizations in your field. As the American Express saying goes, "Membership has its privileges," and being a member can give you access to online jobs before they are made available to the general public.

ACADEMIC HEADHUNTERS

If you haven't been successful in landing a job and feel you can't do it on your own, there is nothing wrong with getting help. Websites such as www.academploy.com/jobs.cfm have a database of recruiters, headhunters, and executive search firms that can assist you. The Association of Executive Search Consultants (www.aesc.org) also has a list of recruiters who can help candidates find academic positions.

Recruiting works in two ways. Recruiters can search for candidates to fill a specific organization's openings, or they can work for you specifically to find an online teaching job. Once you locate an academic recruiter or search firm via an Internet search, ask questions to find out whether there are any fees and who pays them. Many times the hiring company will pay the fees, but ask to make sure.

NEWSPAPERS

Print media are still a popular way to advertise. Even though hiring officials must pay for this form of soliciting applications, posting job announcements in national or local newspapers is a great means of getting a group of diverse candidates. Depending on its circulation, a newspaper advertisement can publicize a job opening to thousands of people. The Sunday edition normally has the largest job section. If you don't want to pay for the newspaper, you can always view it at many local libraries or check out the online versions.

Spending a little time each week reviewing the employment section of a newspaper can pay off. I still see many online teaching jobs listed in the employment section of my local newspaper. They might not be specifically under education but under specialty areas such as accounting, engineering, or business. When trying to land an online teaching job, use all the available resources to increase your chances of success.

SUMMARY

1. Use effective search terms to find online teaching jobs.
2. Broaden your search strategy to include various sources such as the Internet, newspapers, and professional/alumni organizations.
3. If you need help, try a headhunter or get a coach.

NOTES

_____

_____

_____

_____

ACTION STEPS

_____

_____

_____

_____

Step 6

Set Yourself Apart from the Pack

———◈·⋙·◈———

If one advances confidently in the direction of one's dreams,
and endeavors to live the life which one has imagined, one will
meet with a success unexpected in common hours.
— Henry David Thoreau

Believe and act as if it is impossible to fail.
— Charles F. Kettering

Since the goal is to find an online teaching job, you must demonstrate that you know your way around the technology used to facilitate, develop, and administer online education. Remember that those seeking to fill vacancies are looking for candidates who have experience in using technology and are current in that knowledge base.

Fundamental knowledge of word-processing and presentation software is standard. Packages like Microsoft Word and PowerPoint are widely used in the online education environment. You should also be familiar with various equipment such as laptops, webcameras, and Internet connection options (WiFi, DSL high-speed cable). For some organizations these tools are employment requirements. Start preparing yourself for the job you want by securing the tools needed to be successful. Let potential employers know that you are ready, willing, and available for online teaching opportunities. This chapter addresses several ways to demonstrate your technological and online expertise.

CREATE A PERSONAL WEBSITE

Many professionals have at least a one-page website, which is used as the equivalent of a business card. Such sites might contain a picture and biographical profile, including professional experience, hardware and software capabilities, and previous courses taught or training sessions administered. Your personal website should also indicate the highest level of education achieved and your professional-development activities.

You might include as well a statement of professional objectives to let potential employers know the kinds of jobs in which you are interested. I have seen sites that feature client testimonies about how well an instructor facilitated a particular class, program, or assignment. Remember to keep it professional. Highlight your strengths and how they will benefit an organization. Include any videos that show you facilitating classes or serving as a presenter. You also should include professional blogs and links to your professional affiliations.

The website you share with potential employers or set up for professional use is not for your friends. Do not connect it to any of your personal sites. Be sure to keep the backgrounds, pictures, wording, and other elements clear and effective. Use words that will help you secure the job of your dreams. If you need help with phrasing, see the list of résumé buzz-words in Chapter 4. Recruiters and hiring officials use the Internet to conduct searches for potential candidates before they even make a phone call. Ensure that your Internet profile contains details of the professional skills, experience, and knowledge that you will use in the classroom to achieve an organization's mission and goals.

You don't have to spend money to have a personal website. Programs such as Wix.com, yahoo.com, and google.com allow you to create a one-page website for free. You can also create a free blog by using Wordpress. Get your name out there, show what you bring to the table, and let hiring officials know that you understand technology and how to use those elements in the virtual classroom.

CREATE PROFESSIONAL SOCIAL-NETWORKING PAGES

Facebook (facebook.com), Myspace (myspace.com), and Twitter (twitter.
com) can also be used to promote your professional career. You can create
pages that contain a professional bio just as on your professional website.
However, do not allow these professional pages to accept friends or include
any personal information you would not want seen by a potential employer
or client. Be sure, finally, to update such networking pages frequently.

MAKE A VIDEO

Hiring officials need instructors who can use online technology to make
learning effective. Videos offer students the advantage of not only hearing
the instruction but also playing it back until the message is understood.
Online videos demonstrate your commitment to extending learning, since
they can be accessed long after a course is over. You can use online videos
to post lectures, provide feedback on assignments, document your expertise
on various subjects, or demonstrate how to do something. The possibilities
are endless. All you need is a web cam and online video-hosting service.

You can use free hosting services such as Youtube, Stage6, or Grouper
to upload and store your educational videos, as all as Windows Movie
Maker and Audacity to turn slide presentations into movies for uploading
to the Internet.

The next time you teach a class, record it and post it to your professional
website. You also can make money by creating how-to videos for companies
such as eHow.com, answer.com, and about.com. Each of these venues help
people to remember your name and get your application moved to the top
of the pile.

CREATE A BLOG

A blog is an online space for chronological entries that can highlight
your expertise, provide answers to questions, or showcase your projects.
It also allows readers to post comments or ask questions to which you
can respond. A blog thus simulates an online teaching environment by
demonstrating your ability to facilitate a course or even develop one. A
blog allows you to give feedback to readers at all levels.

Demonstrating your technological skills and subject-area knowledge doesn't cost you anything but time. Applications such as blogger.com and wordpress.com allow you to create a free blog. They are easy to set up so that you can get going today.

Host a Webinar, Teleclass, or Teleseminar

If you want to share your expertise with others, hosting a webinar or teleclass is an excellent way to demonstrate your skills to potential employers and let students come to you. Take the time to tell participants about yourself and what they will gain from your instruction. Then outline the topic so that attendees know what to expect during the course. Be engaging. Remember before you end the course to get testimonials for use on your professional and social-network sites. Use free services such as freeconferencecalling.com and freeconferencepro.com to host your classes.

Before you create your own teleseminar, go to www.freeteleseminarlist.com to find a list of free teleseminars on topics of interest. Take notes; then create and host your own. Hosting your own classes will give you experience to add to your résumé and application packet.

Go Back to School

Take additional credit hours in your content area. Most postsecondary schools require at least 18 credit hours in the subject you wish to teach, so if you want to teach on the college level and don't have the credit hours, get them. Not only will you learn the most recent best practices in your field, but taking additional courses will also give you access to educators who might have information about online teaching opportunities.

Introduce yourself to professors in your department as well as chairs and deans. Don't miss out on a great opportunity to be known by insiders who handle the recommending or hiring process.

Make Yourself Visible

Have you ever heard the saying that it's not what you know but who you know? When you are competing with thousands of others for online teaching jobs, it can't hurt if people know your name and credentials. Start making your presence known. Here are a few ways to do so.

Be regarded as a leading expert.

Get your name in print. If you are a subject-area expert, get published by online knowledge bases such as eHow.com, About.com, and Ask.com. Every day millions of people use the Internet to find answers to common questions, and your article can be just what they need. You not only will be paid for your commentary but also will be considered a published expert, having your name and bio in another search engine for prospective employers to find. Networking possibilities with other subject-area experts will ensue.

Be a guest expert on radio or television.

Do you have a topic for which you are a subject-matter expert? Then become a guest specialist on radio or television. Websites such as radioguestlist.com provide a list of shows seeking guests with specific expertise. Blogtalkradio.com inventories thousands of shows that might need your expertise. Conduct a search for shows in your area of interest; then email the host or contact person to ask whether they are seeking guest experts.

What I love about being a guest on Internet radio is that you can do it from the comfort of your home so long as you have access to a phone or the Internet. Although in most cases there is no remuneration, what you get in return for your time is an invaluable networking tool—a recorded interview or podcast that you can post on professional sites to demonstrate your expertise. When hiring officials conduct an Internet search on your name, they will find the radio interviews with a brief bio attached. This is free marketing and professional exposure at its best.

Go where the people are.

Online educators attend professional meetings not only in their specific fields but also in online and distance education. Conferences such as the annual one on Distance Learning and Training or that of the United States Distance Learning Association are helpful venues. There you can meet major players who can give you information about online teaching opportunities. If those conferences don't work for you, set up a conference alert at www.conferencealerts.com. If you choose elearning conferences, you will receive an email list of upcoming distance-education events.

SUMMARY

1. Make yourself visible by using technology to be regarded as an expert.
2. Take advantage of free web resources such as Facebook, LinkedIn and Twitter to network with others in your field.
3. Make a video or be an expert radio guest to demonstrate your experience and skills.

NOTES

_____

_____

_____

_____

_____

_____

ACTION STEPS

_____

_____

_____

_____

_____

_____

PART THREE
Land the Job

All that you need to have all that you want will be provided, as if by magic, once you know what you want and do something about it every day. No matter what.
– Mike Dooley

If your ship doesn't come in, swim out to meet it
– Jonathan Winters

Step 7

Take Action and Apply

———⊰•⊱———

What we think or what we know or what we believe is, in the end, of little consequence. The only consequence is what we do.
— John Ruskin

If you get moving, you get motivated. Even random movement will motivate you. — Paul Myers

Before you apply for a job, have all the essential elements detailed in Part Two of this book:

1. Résumé with an effective statement of objective
2. Cover letter or cover email
3. List of references
4. Scanned unofficial transcripts
5. Statement of teaching philosophy
6. Professional email address

These files should be ready to forward electronically. Remember that hiring officials are not only reviewing your application but also evaluating the response time it takes for you to answer emails and provide requested documents. Having the above ready to send will let prospective employers know that you are professional and will devote the same level of effort to students.

Please don't makeup or inflate your abilities. In most cases you will have to demonstrate them during the interview, initial training or subsequent job. Highlight the skills and experience you bring to the table and ensure you are honest about it. If you are applying for a job based on an online posting, deliver your materials via the method specified in the announcement. In today's fast-paced global environment, most recruiters want information delivered electronically using file formats such as Doc, PDF, or RTF. If a recruiter can't read your files, most likely you will not be contacted to send another version, so get it right the first time.

Last but not least, follow the application instructions carefully and provide all required information. If you are applying where there is no announced position, do your best to find the name of the principal contact person so that you can send your application specifically to him or her. Even if the organization doesn't have anything available at the time of application, you can always request that it keep your information on file in case of future openings. No matter which method you use to apply, if you don't hear anything within six months, apply again. The person who reviewed your application originally may no longer be the hiring official. So apply again. What have you got to lose?

Email

At this stage you should have a professional email address. You can get a free email address at gmail.com, msn.com, hotmail.com, or yahoo. com. Make sure the name you chose professionally represents you such as EdwardsC@hotmail.com. The email name should be either your own (e.g., EdwardsC@gmail.com) or that of your profession. Don't use a nickname or something that will not make a good professional impression such as hotbaby105@gmail.com. Because you might not get a second chance so do it right the first time. After you send in your application materials, check your email inbox daily as well as your spam folder so that you don't miss an employer's email reply. Keep in mind that response time matters. Demonstrate your diligence by answering your email within 24 hours. You will find that the 24-hour response rule during the week and 48 hours on the weekend is mandatory for many online educators. Getting into the habit now will make you all the more ready to teach online.

Direct Contact

Don't hesitate to call hiring officials in the field in which you want to teach, train, or educate. Most companies now have websites that include not only departmental information but also the names, phone numbers, or emails of personnel. The list of online schools in the appendix is a great place to begin. Type organizations' website addresses into your browser and begin researching points of contact.

Before you make calls, gather your thoughts regarding what you will say so that you can detail not only your skills and experience but also your knowledge of the organization and how you can assist in accomplishing its mission and goals. If you haven't already prepared your introductory email, do it now. Demonstrate your availability and the strength of your credentials.

Once you are ready with an introductory email or statement, you can make the call or send the email. If you get a voice mail, leave a brief message that includes your name, telephone number, and email address. Lastly, when sending emails to contact persons, make sure that you have an effective subject line. Indicate what the email is about and what you bring to the table. Here is an example:

Dr. Edwards - Over ten years of online business teaching experience available for online assignments

This subject line lets the reader know that the sender is experienced, has a doctorate, and is ready for online assignments in the business area. You could also accomplish the same thing with this subject line:

John Jones, M.S.A., available to teach online music courses

This subject line provides the candidate's name, level of education, and area of specialization. A clear and simple subject line helps the reader know what to do with the email. Ensure that your emails get noticed by using a short but effective subject line.

ONLINE APPLICATION SYSTEMS

Some organizations will not accept applications by either email or snail mail whether or not they have openings. Most application procedures are outlined in an announcement. Online screening systems allow employers to have a searchable database of applicants with corresponding education and skill levels. In many cases you will be directed to fill out an online application form. This recruiting tool not only is good for the employer but also allows applicants to view specific job openings and their requirements.

Online systems allow you to set up job alerts as well. You can access an employer's online job site detailed in the position announcement to search the company's database for criteria. Input your email address to receive alerts when specific types of openings are available. Setting up an online alert allows the jobs to come to you. You then can submit your stored online application or résumé within seconds of receiving a job announcement.

Using automated job alerts and applying quickly can help you get noticed by potential employers. The dean of a community college stated, "If you wait for a specific job opening, you might be too late." So be proactive and set up an online profile that contains your résumé, cover letter, and references since there is a good chance that recruiters will pick candidates from their databases. Below are some examples of jobs that require you to apply using online application systems. Remember that these links are from previously open positions and most likely are no longer active.

Online Accounting Faculty Position
Contact: Human Resources
Online: App. Form: http://posttrak.arbita.net/cgi-bin/
PostTrak.cgi?RefCode=R9376120510034

Online Statistics Instructor Position
Contact: Interested applicants should visit the following Web address at http://online.argosy.edu/about/employment. aspx and follow the application procedures. All submissions will be acknowledged, and review of applicants will begin immediately.

Online Teacher Performance Scorer
Contact: Interested applicants should fill out electronic application at: https://vovici.com/wsb.dll/s/6bf3g4d59e.

Online Curriculum Developer
Contact: Relay Graduate School of Education
Phone: 212-228-1888
Online App. Form: http://relayschool.org
Email Address: jobs@relayschool.org

COLD CALLING

Use the Internet as a research tool to find people who hire for the areas in which you wish to work. In most instances colleges, universities, and educational organizations have a website that contains phone numbers or email addresses for specific people in Human Resources or at least general information on the hiring department. It's called "cold calling" when you don't know the person you are contacting or whether there is an actual job opening. To find potential contacts, I suggest conducting a Google search for online schools or using the list of schools with online programs in the appendix. I would then click on each school to make sure it has programs of interest. You can also find this information at www.directoryofschools. com.

You can search for online schools or specific programs by subject. Don't limit yourself only to schools. Conduct Internet searches for vocations that might be education-related such as publishing or IT companies. You will be surprised at the number of opportunities available to educate online. As I've said more than once, the positions truly are out there.

For each organization find the number of the dean, recruiter, or even admissions personnel. Start calling and asking about open positions. Send your application packet to specific contacts. Remember to revise the cover letter to include the name, address, phone number, and email of the person to whom you are sending the information. There's nothing worse than sending a cover letter with the wrong recipient's information. Take your time and do it right. Keep in mind that sending an impressive and error-free application can set you apart from other candidates.

Professional Organizations and Meetings

I am a member of the Academy of Management, a professional association for scholars who want to share and learn about the discipline of management. These types of organizations exist for almost every discipline. Not only can you attend yearly conferences that may include a job fair, but you also can submit papers or presentation topics. This is a great way to network and get your name out there. You also can sign up for specific online groups in which you are interested. I cannot tell you how many job openings are sent to members of the Academy of Management groups to which I belong. This is an efficient way to get your application materials directly to a recruiter or hiring official.

Many positions are first advertised internally, so knowing people on the inside allows you to fast-track your application. One dean at a community college stated, "I find many candidates at professional organizations because the members share the same interests and have the minimum education or experience requirements." Use your networks at these professional organizations to let others know of your credentials and availability. Have business cards ready to exchange with those of contacts. Then follow up!

Virtual Career Fairs

Business leaders have found that they can save the expense of renting space and tables for face-to-face career fairs by conducting interviews over the Internet. You can meet prospective employers via online video services such as Skype and speak to hiring officials in real time. You also can post your résumé to the specified virtual link, have it evaluated by hiring officials, and receive a call or email if they are interested. Recently a virtual career fair was held for online educators at http://expos2events. com/onlinefaculty/ to help job-seekers network with college and university personnel. Live communication was conducted through chat and webcam. This is just one more way to use technology to get your résumé noticed and to demonstrate your skills in using technology.

Advertisements

Some companies still take the time to post job announcements in local and national newspapers. Although these practices still take place, according to one dean, "Most of the positions are announced through electronic means." So if you find a job announcement in a newspaper, have your application materials ready to send. Many employers seeking online educators require the ability to use online resources, so that, even if an announcement appears in print venues, more than likely you will still submit your application via an online system or email. No matter the mode of advertising, demonstrating adeptness in the use of technology is still a factor.

Summary

1. Make sure your application has all the required information.
2. Send applications using the preferred method.
3. Seek out jobs by contacting points of contact.
4. Stay in the loop by joining professional organizations.
5. If you hear nothing back, apply again in six months.

Notes

_____

_____

_____

_____

_____

Action Steps

_____

_____

_____

_____

_____

Step 8

Believe You Can Have It

————◆◆◆◆————

*We can have whatever it is that we choose. I
don't care how big it is. — John Assaraf*

*It's the repetition of affirmations that leads to belief. And once
that belief becomes a deep conviction, things begin to happen.
— Muhammad Ali*

Have you ever wondered why some people always come out on top, seem
to land on their feet even when things look grim, or have a job during an
economic recession? The ability to believe that you can have what you want
is pivotal in securing an online job. Even though there are many applicants,
or you don't see the perfect job listed online, you still must believe that you
can land an assignment. Take some time to consider those who have been
successful and what they did to press on when things looked bleak.

Millionaires like Wayne Dyer, Lisa Nichols, Joe Vitale, and Oprah
Winfrey have overcome huge odds to live the life of their dreams. If you
read their biographies, you will find that they all had a faith that they
could attain what they wanted. People often ask me how my husband and I
moved from Washington, D.C., and found jobs in Miami during the worst
economic recession I can remember. The answer is simple: we stepped out
in faith and believed we could do it.

We must focus our mind's energy on what we want to happen, what we want to achieve, and how we want to live. Doing so will help the universe to conspire with you in bringing the right people, circumstances, and opportunities to propel you toward an online teaching position. Ask yourself these questions:

- Do you believe that you can work online and make money at it?

- Do you feel that you have the requisite education, tools, and experience?

- Are you positive about your abilities to teach online and do a great job?

- Do you trust that the right opportunity will present itself at exactly the right time?

- Do you believe that you are prepared to seize opportunities as they arise?

On the other hand, ask yourself these questions:

- Do you believe that you won't get chosen because thousands of people are trying to get the same online job as you are?

- Do you believe that there aren't any available jobs online that need your skill set?

- Do you think that everyone else except you has the inside track on landing an online job?

- Do you heed naysayers' advice not to waste your time?

- Do you think that all the available jobs have been taken?

If you answered yes to the first set of questions, your thinking is on track to get you what you want. If not, you might want to devote some time to believing and trusting that you can land an online educator job.

Many career gurus talk about the psychology of belief and how the mind's energy will help you to realize your dreams. James Ray, author of

The Science of Success, thus remarks: "You should know what you want and think about those things. Use your thoughts to get a clear mental picture of the exact results you want to achieve and think about that." Remember that your beliefs have power and that you usually get exactly what you expect. So why not use your energy to envision yourself teaching online and experiencing the joy of working from home? Discussed below are some proven tools to help you secure an online job.

Establish a Vision

Create an overall vision statement that describes your online career. The statement helps you to understand exactly what it is you want. Do you wish to work full-time online from home, be an adjunct professor, or perhaps an online high-school teacher? Would you like to develop your own online courses? Your vision statement will give direction on how to focus your search efforts. The following definition from timethoughts.com sums it up excellently: "A vision statement is a vivid idealized description of a desired outcome that inspires, energizes, and helps you to create a mental picture of your target."

According to Bob Proctor in his book titled *It's Not About the Money*, "Every time you think something, you're putting energy in motion. Positive thoughts are magnets for more positive energy." Establish a vision of what you want to achieve. It will be a map that keeps you on course when things don't seem to be going your way. Doing just one thing each day to move you in the direction of achieving your goal can help you to achieve it.

Set Goals

Determine the type of online job you want to have. Do you want to work for a university, college, or high school? Do you want to teach or be an online administrator? Setting specific goals keeps you focused. It also helps you to develop action steps for staying on track.

Action steps can be as simple as reviewing online job sites in the appendix, developing a list of companies where you want to work, or making a call to a former professor to inquire about job openings. Just remember to do something each day to move you one step closer to teaching online.

AFFIRM

Positive words in the present tense help you to believe that what you want to happen will happen. Affirmations help you believe that you are worthy of getting what it is you want and assist in putting your mind in a state of expectation to receive it. You can vocalize the words by saying them out loud or you can write them down and read them. No matter the method you choose, you should repeat the words several times throughout the day. Some common affirmations for landing an online job are:

- I love teaching classes online from home.

- Earning a six-figure salary for teaching online is great.

- I'm amassing great wealth by teaching online.

- Teaching online gives me the freedom to travel.

- My online career is successful and abundant.

- There is a huge online demand for my skills and abilities.

- I am successful in educating online.

Affirming that you have what you want can help you to achieve your goals at a faster rate.

VISUALIZE

Consciously use your imagination to see yourself educating online in the environment of your choice like working from home or sitting on the beach with your laptop. Close your eyes and imagine yourself facilitating an online class. Feel the joy of working in your shorts or pajamas. Include details such as your physical work location (e.g., home, local coffee shop, or library). Even when you feel doubtful, continue to invoke your mental picture. Shakti Gawain in her book titled *Creative Visualization* remarks, "Consciously imagining what we want can help us to manifest it in our lives." Use this technique to secure an online teaching job.

Seek Help

You don't have to go it alone. There are many professional groups on the Internet such as LinkedIn and Facebook where you can request advice and network with those in your field. Many colleges and universities offer career advice and assistance to alumni, so go back to your alma mater and seek assistance.

Be Persistent

Many anecdotes in this book come from those who did not get the first online teaching job they sought. At one university it took me almost three years to land a teaching position. Eventually I was hired because I never gave up. Neither did many others in this book. Develop a job search schedule. A good rule of thumb is to apply for a position at least two to three times per week.

Learn from Experience

As you develop a winning application, learn from the experience to hone your skills. For example, I learned to make sure that I proofread everything I submitted. I once created an application letter while on vacation and distracted by all the activity around me. I didn't take the time to make sure that my wording communicated how I could address the company's needs spelled out in the position description.

After a month without even an automated reply, I reread my application letter, in which I found many mistakes. Thereafter I made sure that every document I sent out was a true reflection of my professionalism. You might not get it right the first time, but learn from each experience and do better going forward.

Ask for the Job

When you send out an application or speak with a hiring official, don't forget to ask for the job. When I develop a cover letter or email, I ask for what I want right up front. Timothy Flood in *Business Writing* recommends putting the most important information in the opening paragraph. This approach lets the reader know immediately the document's purpose. When you tell the reader what you want at the beginning, he or she doesn't have to guess. In this regard I love what Mahatma Gandhi once said: "If you don't ask, you don't get."

Don't Be Afraid of No

If you don't receive a favorable reply to your application package, don't give up. Apply to other schools or organizations. If you don't get hired by one, you might get hired by the next prospect. A rejection can help you to understand what is not working in your résumé or application materials. If you have a contact name for the job you were seeking, call him or her and ask what you can do the next time to make your application the chosen one.

The word "NO" can provide the opportunity to analyze your skills and discover areas where you might need additional training, education, or expertise in order to turn "NO" into "YES." Getting a "NO" was probably why you picked up this book and are now learning the steps to teach online successfully.

Give Back

Often we think of ourselves when trying to get an online job, but your application should let employers know what is in it for them. Appeal to the interests of the company and explain how you can meet their needs. Talk, of course, about all the great things you can do, but if there is not an immediate opening offer your services for free. Volunteer to teach a class. You also can offer to write an article for the school's newsletter, provide career-specific resources or handouts to students, deliver a free webinar or teleseminar, and participate in the organization's blog. Jack Canfield, author of the *Chicken Soup* series, says, "When you're nice to people, they want to be nice back to you."

Offering to help the company for free not only let's people know that you are an expert in your field but that you are willing to go above and beyond other applicants to help the organization achieve its mission. Volunteering gets your name noticed and remembered.

Keep Track of Your Successes

If you teach a course, seminar, or webinar, always make sure that you solicit evaluations from attendees and supervisors. These will be beneficial for your application packet and professional networking websites. They also will be reminders that you are on the right track to achieving your goals. I have a large White Board directly on the wall in front of my desk that features a list of the successes I accomplished during the year. It helps me to stay motivated and reminds me that I am doing my best to help others achieve their dreams.

Summary

1. Focus each day on the result you want.
2. Visualize yourself at your desk working online or anywhere in the world you want to work. See yourself at the beach conducting a class or seminar or in the park writing a textbook chapter.
3. Don't worry about how it will happen; just trust that it will. Don't get bogged down in distracting details.
4. Keep applying, researching, and networking to teach online.
5. Give of yourself to help meet the needs of others and document your successes as you continue to get noticed.

Notes

_____

_____

_____

_____

Action Steps

_____

_____

_____

_____

Step 9

Ask, Then Ask Again

You've got to ask! Asking is, in my opinion, the world's most powerful—and neglected—secret to success and happiness. –
Percy Ross

To solve any problem, here are three questions to ask yourself:
First, what could I do? Second, what could I read? And third,
who could I ask? – Jim Rohn

As Anthony Robbins has said, "Success leaves clues." If you want to know how those successfully educating online got their foot in the door, don't hesitate to ask them. Your goal is to get where they are or have been. Because I wanted to help you land an online job, I asked people who are successful to share their insights. Although not everyone was willing to divulge their journey, many were. I figured I had nothing to lose but a whole lot to gain. By asking and not fearing being told "no," I acquired a wealth of information that can guide you in achieving your goal.

How Did They Do It?

It was as simple as asking the same question I've been asked for the past ten years. This question is continually posted in online blogs and groups.

It's especially significant to those who don't have any teaching experience. In one online group a member commented that he had a Ph.D. plus over twenty years of teaching experience and had been applying for the last few years but had not gotten any offers to educate online. Although this person had taught in a campus setting, he wondered why he could not branch off to educate online.

He is not the only one experiencing this problem, which is one reason why I wrote this book. It is not enough to have the right educational background. You still need to demonstrate that you are technologically adept and can meet an organization's goals as well as teach students. It can't hurt to get some online instructional experience. Whether you get the information from a book, research, articles or a person – you should always seek wisdom from those that have come before you and are successful at what you wish to accomplish. Success leaves clues, so consulting those who have been successful at what you wish to accomplish is only prudent. This is what the colleagues I asked had to say about how they landed their jobs.

NETWORK

Develop professional contacts to share resources, information, and opportunities. Each party benefits from the reciprocal relationship. When you attend professional meetings, communicate your goals and exchange business cards with others so that you can keep in touch.

Several colleagues I queried obtained online teaching positions because they asked people in their network of contacts whether they knew of any opportunities. One person noted:

> I was looking for a career change. I had the skills and education to educate online, but I was not successful in just sending my résumé. So I emailed some former coworkers I used to teach with on-site to inquire whether they knew of any openings. I was pleased to find out they knew of several, and I was recommended for a position just because I sought help from those in my network.

Volunteer

Organization leaders know the importance of giving back to the community. Doing so builds good will and also complies with the Community Reinvestment Act. Some organizations adopt schools, while others might partner with nonprofits such as Habitat for Humanity, Race for the Cure, and the American Red Cross. No matter the charity, volunteering is a great way to network and help those in need. One online writer commented:

> I found my job because I volunteered in my church's administrative office. I was working with another volunteer who needed help filling a contract-writing position. After sharing a little about ourselves, she learned that I had a background as a journalist. I sent her my résumé, and that's how I got my first online writing job.

Join Professional Organizations

Many professional organizations not only provide information on specific topics for their members but also distribute job announcements, host job workshops, and arrange opportunities for on-site hiring at annual meetings. Organizations such as the Academy of Management, National Bar Association, Association of Professional Educators, American Association of University Professors, Society of Women Engineers, and others might be the source of your next online teaching position. There are online opportunities in almost every field or specialty.

Join Online Groups

I am a member of quite a few online groups via Yahoo, Facebook, and LinkedIn. I join those in which I have interests such as online educators, authors, consultants, coaches, eteachers, and online adjuncts. My purpose is to keep abreast of what is going on in the industry and to network with others in the field by sharing resources and opportunities.

While in one of my LinkedIn groups this week, I discovered twelve postings for online teaching positions. In addition, a university dean posted a request for applicants. Membership and posting in these groups are free. Such announcements allow organizations to invite the submission of résumés from those affiliated with particular online groups. One LinkedIn participant noted:

> I sent my résumé to the request link posted within the group. I was contacted, interviewed, and hired within a few months of sending the résumé. Working together with online colleagues helped me get my foot in the door.

You can also have your name added to the list of adjuncts at http://www.adjunctworld.com. Joining the list allows you to network with others in the field as well as to receive emails concerning job openings. Recruiters can browse the list and select you based on your skills profiled in the directory.

Tutor

Some seeking to obtain online employment have served as tutors. This form of teaching can be arranged on either a volunteer or compensated basis. An online educator posted the following:

> I worked in the tutoring office as a program assistant and tutor. The work helped me to get an internship and then use that experience to get a professional position. Even part-time jobs can help you to meet people and get your foot in the door. Many work/study students are hired later.

Teach Summer Courses

Experienced online educators know that in the summer months many regular faculty like to take vacations. This provides opportunities for others to come in on a temporary basis to instruct. An online course developer commented:

> I was able to get a temporary position as a course designer while the regular designer was off due to medical leave. This allowed me to learn different systems, gain more experience, and have access to management staff in the company. The temporary experience turned into a full-time online position.

Work On-Site First

Sometimes working for an organization on campus, in the office, or at a satellite location is the way to begin. In many cases online personnel stated that they were offered a position because they were already employed by an organization. An online educator remarked:

> Many job openings are posted on internal employee systems. Jobs are offered internally first before they are advertised outside the organization. This is how I was able to get my foot into the online teaching door. I started teaching on campus first.

Learn to Play Golf

Many organizations sponsor charity events such as golf tournaments. Early in my professional career during the 1990s I took golf lessons because networking, business deals, and hiring decisions occurred on the golf course. Not much has changed since then.

Professional organizations still sponsor charity golf events. Just a few months ago one online school where I work had a tournament in which you could bring others to play in your foursome. This would have been a great opportunity for someone seeking entry into the industry to play golf and meet decision-makers. One online educator offered this comment:

> I was invited to a charity golf tournament where I met many higher-education administrators. It provided the opportunity to learn about the university culture and its online opportunities.

Meet the Principal Contacts

Making face-to-face contact lets prospective employers know who you are and how you can benefit an organization. Since most applications are completed online and without personal interaction with officials or recruiters, meeting them allows both parties to put a face with the name and email address. It also allows you to elaborate on your skills, goals, and technological expertise. One online employee remarked:

Talk to the people who can help. I got an offer to teach as an adjunct by going to the university, looking up the dean of its business school, and inquiring about online opportunities.

Meeting in person with the hiring staff and department managers demonstrates that you are willing to go the extra mile to be an asset to their institution.

Answer a Newspaper or Magazine Ad

Although many seeking applicants take advantage of free advertising via online groups, social-networking sites, and internal postings, scores of companies continue to advertise in print media. Applying for a job advertised in a newspaper or magazine might seem antiquated, but many have done it with success. An online educator stated:

I applied for a job I saw in my local newspaper. To my surprise I was interviewed and offered the position.

Attend Professional Meetings

Attend courses, conferences, and professional meetings sponsored by organizations that you know have online positions. Put yourself in proximity to those who can assist in your job search. One online group participant said:

I found a job at a university by attending a professional conference where I was giving a workshop for graduate students. Generally at conferences university officials try to recruit students to come to their schools, but I was trying to get them to invite me to teach. Luckily for me the dean was at the same conference and mentioned that she was looking for someone with my skill set.

Follow Up

Many times it's not enough to send in your application or apply online. Hiring officials have to sort through hundreds of résumés to get the right candidate. Make yourself stand out by sending a thank-you note or follow up with an email. An online educator commented:

> I applied online through the organization's website, but after a month or so I didn't hear back from them, so I met with the hiring official in person. I wanted them to put a face with my credentials, and I wanted to meet the people I would work for and with. This helped me to get the job because they remembered my extra effort.

SHARE YOUR GOALS

When engaged in casual conversation, tell people not only what you're doing now but also what your future aspirations are. You never know who can move you one step closer to your goal. One educator observed:

> Some of my best jobs have come from general conversations. Just telling someone what I do for a living and what I want to do in the future have led to someone's giving me a phone number or email of a contact person who could help.

ASK YOUR PROFESSOR

If you are currently taking classes, your professor can be a wonderful resource. According to Shakti Gawain, "You create your opportunities by asking for them," so don't hesitate to ask. An online instructor remarked:

> I spoke with a professor and expressed my dissatisfaction with agency work and my desire to teach as an adjunct. The professor gave me the name of a contact at the school. I emailed that person; we met; and I was offered an adjunct online position.

GET ONLINE EXPERIENCE

Even though you might have teaching experience, some organizations prefer that you have *online* experience. This begs the second most frequently asked question posted in online groups and blogs:

"How do you get online educator experience if you can't get the online job first?"

Here are several ways to gain such experience.

Substitute for others. Years ago one of the online institutions for which I worked allowed us to bring in substitutes when we were not able to teach a session. I had to provide the person's résumé and references, but the substitute was approved based on her education and experience. She was able to put this experience on her résumé, helping her to land an opportunity facilitating an online course. Substitute-teaching policies differ from one organization to another, so check regulations before you allow anyone without permission access to company information or systems.

Volunteer. Nonprofit organizations might not have the money to sponsor a class, but in many cases they are happy to have local professionals teach a free community-based course. You can teach all sorts of classes in computer literacy, business, communication, résumé-building, or critical thinking. You might not get a salary, but you can get noticed. Volunteering demonstrates your willingness to be involved in your local community. An online colleague commented:

> I am a certified financial planner who approached my local library to teach others how to manage credit. I had about 30 people in the initial course, and it went so well that I was invited to conduct this training several times throughout the year. I took this course to the Internet and conducted a teleseminar using the same information. This experience helped me to get my feet wet, and from that experience I was confident enough to take the training to an online environment and then use that experience to get my first online job teaching finance.

Become familiar with Learning Management Systems. There are many opportunities to gain experience with various online teaching systems. Some are even free. Here are a few links for courses and tutorials that can enhance your skills and experience.

Introduction to Easy Campus
http://www.easycampuslearn. com/

Moodle Courses and Resources
http://moodlecommons.org/
http://moodle-tutorials.blogspot.com/

Blackboard Tutorials
http://ondemand.blackboard.com/r9/index.htm
http://blackboardinfo.newark.rutgers.edu/tutorials.html

eCollege Tutorials
http://cite.nwmissouri.edu/ic/ecollegetutorial/index.html
http://cite.nwmissouri.edu/ic/ecollegetutorial/index.html
http://academics.smcvt.edu/eCollege/Archive/Tutorial_
Basics1.htm

Desire2Learn Tutorials
https://itascacc.ims.mnscu.edu/shared/MnScuStudent
Tutorials/MnSCUOrientVideos.html
http://teachingcommons.depaul.edu/Technology/d2l/index.html

Websites such as www.mastersandmasters.com, facultytraining.net, and www.marylandonline.org/coat offer courses or certificates that will give you experience in online education. You can use the credentials you earn to strengthen your résumé. See more online educator courses in the appendix.

Create an online tutorial. You can make a video with your webcam and upload it to sites such as www.youtube.com or www.myspace.com for free. I use many business-related YouTube videos in my courses in order to get noticed. You can also put the links on your professional pages to demonstrate your skills.

Be seen as an expert. Make presentations at your current job, office, or library using technology such as Screencast, PowerPoint, and Jing. The goal is to demonstrate your proficiency in using technology to enhance learning. One colleague of mine remarked:

> I attend a monthly community business meeting and I gave a presentation on how to manage your finances during a recession.

The dean of the local community college was in attendance and after the session asked me about teaching the same class at the college. When I first started, the course was in the Continuing Education program, but this was the stepping stone to teaching finance and accounting classes online.

Develop a blog. A blog is a self-marketing tool that allows others to recognize your communication and technical skills. A blog allows you to advertise your skills. On it you can include links to your professional website and videos to convince prospective recruiters of what you can do for their companies. An online educator commented:

> I've received great feedback and responsiveness to my teaching blog. People have posted questions about my teaching journey, and I've been able to help not only myself but a few educators get online jobs. It is definitely worth spending a few hours each week posting to the blog.

SUMMARY

1. You don't have to reinvent the wheel. Learn from those already in online education.
2. Get additional training if necessary.
3. Demonstrate your adeptness at using technology.
4. Show your expertise by creating presentations, videos, and blogs.

NOTES

ACTION STEPS

Step 10

Keep Moving

———◆◆◆◆———

*Always bear in mind that your own resolution to succeed is
more important than any other. – Abraham Lincoln*

*There are no secrets to success. It is the result of preparation,
hard work, and learning from failure. – Colin Powell*

Now that you have read these chapters and determined that teaching
online is for you, take action. Don't give up on your long-term goals.
Here are some techniques to keep you motivated, organized, and moving
forward while waiting on your first online teaching job.

KEEP A LIST

It is important to remember when you applied for every available position.
When recruiters contact you, you want to know what you sent and to
whom and the type of job sought. Putting all of this information in a
Word table, Excel spreadsheet, or any other record-keeping method will
help you to be ready when an employment offer comes. Here are some
items to include in your list:

- Application date

- Organization's name

- Point of contact

- Application method (if online, list the username and password)

- Material sent

- Feedback received

- Follow-up response

- Results

The list not only keeps you motivated but also serves as a means to gather additional information about what didn't work so that you can be more successful the next time. See the job sheet in the appendix for an example.

FOLLOW-UP

If there is no feedback within six months, reapply or follow up. Doing so lets contacts know that you are serious about an assignment. It helps you to stand out from the crowd of others who just fill out the application but never call, visit, or send a follow-up inquiry about their applications' status.

BE RESPONSIVE

Be ready when potential employers come looking for you. In most cases you will be sent an email, so check your email inbox and spam folders daily. When you get an email, respond quickly. Recruiters for online teaching assignments want instructors who respond promptly to email communications. Most likely you must respond to the client email within 48 to 36 hours. If you respond after that time frame, they will most likely have contacted the applicant next in line.

A colleague was once contacted by a large online school. She really wanted the online job and had applied several times over a few years. However when she got the email requesting she complete several forms and return them, she did not respond until seven days later. Needless to say, the school never contacted her again. She has been applying for the last few years, without any success.

I suggest that you respond no later than 48 hours after any requests. Even if you can't immediately provide the requested documents, at least acknowledge that you received the request and are actively working on it.

Clean Up Your Personal Websites

Hiring officials search the internet for potential candidates. This search includes all sites not just professional ones. If you don't think potential employers can get your personal photographs and writings, think again.

There have been quite a few instructors, professors and teachers in the news recently who have lost jobs due to unprincipled pictures, musings, thoughts or opinions found on social networking sites. In many cases instructors are held to high moral standards since they are examples of professionalism for students. If there is information that you would never want an employer to see, I suggest removing it or ensure that is it securely password protected. My motto is when in doubt, leave it out.

Be Professional

Take your job and job hunt seriously. Answer emails quickly, be timely in responses to peers and colleagues and always submit deliverables that you want to represent your skills and abilities. If you commit to something, make it happen. When you can't fulfill your obligations, communicate before the deadline so other options can be explored.

Many years ago I had an opportunity to interview for a job. I didn't want to commute to the job location, so instead of declining the interview I didn't show up. A few weeks later the perfect job was posted that was close to home and paid more than the previous opportunity. I called to inquire about the new opening, but once the recruiter heard my name she asked,

"Weren't you supposed to have an interview a few weeks ago?" I didn't get the job I wanted. Always treat people the way you want to be treated.

Learn How to Ask

How will the recruiter know if you really want the job if you don't ask? Even before you receive an interview make sure that before you end the application, cover letter or email that you ask for the job. You might be thinking I don't want to be too pushy or aggressive but why not use a proactive approach to getting what you want. Without risk you can't get the reward.

Asking sets you apart from those that passively submit applications. Asking communicates enthusiasm, eagerness and willingness to be a part of the team or organization.

Some common phrases you can use to ask for the job are:

- I look forward to working with you.

- I look forward to our working together.

- I can't wait to be an asset to the company.

- I would really like to teach at XYZ Company.

- The company is a great match.

- This job is perfect for my skills and experience. I'd really like to work with you.

- I'm very interested in this job.

Establish a Profile on LinkedIn.com

This free networking site gets thousands of new members each week. It allows you to extend your online outreach. One hiring official stated:

I check LinkedIn to see if a potential candidate is listed. It allows me to find out more background and data on the candidate before I schedule an interview.

Stay Current with Professional Development

While you are awaiting a response from prospective employers, keep current on your professional development. Take a class, write a blog, attend a conference, or deliver a presentation. Continually staying abreast of your career field makes you marketable in the eyes of recruiters. Since most accredited schools, if that is the route you want to pursue, require a certain amount of continuing education or professional development each year, it makes sense to keep your skills current. This book's appendix contains a list of companies that help you to establish Learning Management Systems (LMS) experience.

Interview Effectively

Your job interviews will probably be over the phone with one or several people on a conference call. Toward the end of the interview, be sure to say that you are ready to do the work and, last but not least, ask for the job. Use such language as the following: "When can I expect to hear from you?" "I look forward to working with you," and "I am truly excited about this job opportunity."

Don't forget to jot down your interview on a contact list and then follow up with an email or phone call if you don't hear anything within a few weeks. The best method is email because you will have a record of the message. If you have the capability on your email system, remember to get a confirmation that the recipient read your message.

Don't Focus Only on Money

If an offer is not for as much pay as you had hoped, don't make a decision based only on that factor. Pay is just one area you should consider when searching for schools and organizations where you want to work. If you do not have prior online teaching experience or are starting with a master's or bachelor's degree, I suggest you focus your search efforts on tutoring, career schools, two-year colleges, and private organizations, which seem to be more willing to hire someone without prior online experience. However, the pay at these schools probably is lower than what you might receive at a four-year university or graduate program. Why is that? Because most graduate courses are taught by those with a Ph.D. or comparable degree who have many years of online or face-to-face teaching experience. Their level of compensation is thus usually commensurate with what they are bringing to the table in terms of qualifications.

Of course there are exceptions to every rule, but for most of those I've coached who did not have prior online teaching experience; their first job was with a two-year school, career college, or private organization. Remember even though the pay might not be as high as you would like, there are other benefits such as the following:

- Entrance into the online teaching arena

- Opportunity to network with hiring officials, deans, department chairs, etc.

- Opportunity to teach effectively and get noticed

- Online teaching experience

- Experience with learning systems such as Blackboard, eCollege, Angel, Moodle, and Desire2Learn

- Access to student evaluations of your teaching performance

- Free professional development or association memberships since some organizations pay for these instructor benefits

Use the above benefits to propel you into higher-paying positions. Remember that teaching online is a journey, not a sprint. We all had to start somewhere. Obtaining your first online teaching assignment will yield a great deal of benefits other than salary.

REVIEW YOUR RÉSUMÉ

As you wait on receiving your first or second online assignment, make sure that your application packet effectively details what you can bring to the company. Your résumé should highlight any teaching experience and the specific courses taught. Showcase all the LMS technology with which you are familiar such as eCollege, Blackboard, and Angel, as well as teaching tools such as Jing, Screencast, and Microsoft Office.

Lastly, if you have a full-time job or several part-time ones, make certain that your résumé does not make you look too busy or overworked. Hiring officials want to know that their students and clients will be a priority. Adjunct teaching jobs should be listed on an "as needed" basis since there is no guarantee of employment from term to term. This qualifying phrase lets hiring officials know that you have time to focus on their clients and needs.

BE CONFIDENT

After you've read and put into practice the tips presented in this book, see yourself doing what you love—teaching online. Fill in the blank lines of the following sentence to help you realize the joy of teaching online. Then copy the page for use as a daily reminder and affirmation of what you will achieve!

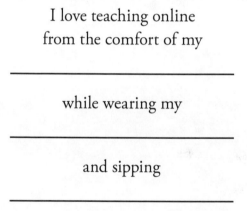

I love teaching online
from the comfort of my

_____

while wearing my

_____

and sipping

_____

Be patient and persistent. Complete the steps in this book knowing you are doing what it takes to achieve your dreams. Focus on the results and what you want your career and work life to look like. You too can be a success and secure an online teaching job! May you land the online educating, teaching, instructional, developer, facilitator, writer, or presenter job of your dreams! Success may not happen overnight. It takes commitment and drive so continue to focus on your goals. Do the work; affirm your goals; have faith; think positively. Then every day *do one thing to move yourself in the direction of achieving your dreams of teaching online.*

NOTES

_____

_____

_____

_____

_____

ACTION STEPS

_____

_____

_____

_____

_____

Contact

If you would like more information on how Dr. Carolyn Edwards can help you land an online teaching job, please visit www.drcarolynedwards.com or theteachonlinebook.com. There you will find articles, blogs, and media as well as free downloads to get you moving in the direction of teaching online.

If you want further information on coaching and training services, please send an email to dre@drcarolynedwards.com or fill out the contact form at www.drcarolynedwards.com.

You also can contact Dr. Edwards at http://www.facebook.com/pages/Dr-Carolyn-Edwards/154950224574565 and follow her blog at www.drcarolynedwards.wordpress.com.

Sample Documents

SAMPLE COVER EMAIL

To: Mary Strong
From: John Doe
Date: December 15, 2011
Subject: Application for Online Business Instructor

Dear Ms. Strong,

This email concerns the Online Business Instructor position advertised on the University of Phoenix's website. My goal is to use my ten years of business and presentation experience as well as my master's degree in business to apply course concepts to real-life situations. I focus on helping students to understand how theory is put into action, which I know is part of the University's mission. (*This opening paragraph tells the reader what you want and what you bring to the table, while making clear that you understand the organization's mission.*)

I am adept at using various methods of training such as PowerPoint, Jing, and the Internet both to develop and to deliver learning modules. During my years of serving as a business director and subject-matter expert, I have coached, counseled, and mentored over 100 employees to become organizational assets. (*This second paragraph sells your skills and matches them to the position. Use facts, numbers, and awards to back up your claims.*)

Thank you for your consideration. I look forward to the opportunity to use my expertise in current business skills for the benefit of students enrolled at the University of Phoenix. (*This final paragraph indicates what you can do for the organization.*)

Respectfully,

John Doe
203-555-1212
johndoe@hotmail.com (*Always include a contact number and email.*)
Attachments: Résumé, References, Transcripts

SAMPLE COVER LETTER

John Doe
1234 Mayoral Avenue
Phoenix, AZ 22334

December 15, 2011

Mary Strong
University of Phoenix
831 West Street
San Francisco, CA 95228

Dear Ms. Strong:

Please consider my application for the Online Business Instructor position advertised on the University of Phoenix's website. My goal is to use my ten years of business and presentation experience as well as my master's degree in business to apply course concepts to real-life situations. I focus on helping students to understand how theory is put into action, which I know is part of the University's mission. *(This opening paragraph tells the reader what you want and what you bring to the table, while making clear that you understand the organization's mission.)*

I am adept at using various methods of training such as PowerPoint, Jing, and the Internet both to develop and to deliver learning modules. During my years of serving as a business director and subject-matter expert, I have coached, counseled, and mentored over 100 employees to become organizational assets. *(This second paragraph sells your skills and matches them to the position. Use facts, numbers, and awards to back up your claims.)*

Thank you for your consideration. I look forward to the opportunity to use my expertise in current business skills for the benefit of students enrolled at the University of Phoenix. *(This final paragraph indicates what you can do for the organization.)*

Respectfully,

John Doe
203-555-1212
johndoe@hotmail.com *(Always include a contact number and email.)*
Attachments: Résumé, References, Transcript

SAMPLE RESUME

John Doe
1234 Mayoral Avenue Phoenix, AZ 22334
203 - 555 – 1212 * johndoe@hotmail.com

Objective: Obtain an online educator position which utilizes the use of fifteen years of business experience and technology, instruction, customer service and instruction skills. *(Ensure objective tells the reader about your skills and the type of job you want)*

Education: *(Make sure you highlight not only postsecondary degrees but also applicable training or certifications)*

- Master of Science – IT 2006 – North Carolina University
- Bachelor of Science – Management 2002 – Alabama State University
- eCollege Certification 2009

Summary of Qualifications: *(Tell the reader what skills, experience and expertise make you an asset to the company, include any specific skills that were outlined in the announcement)*

- Three years of online instructor experience IT and Management courses
- Experienced using eCollege, Moodle, Blackboard, Angel, Screencast, Internet, Microsoft Office

Experience : *(Most employers want the last 5 to 10 years of employment history, make sure you highlight the most sought after skills and experience in your job descriptions)*

Colorado College, Washington, DC
Adjunct Professor, (2009-Present)

- Conduct undergraduate lectures, develop course curriculum, create PowerPoint based tutorials, exams and lectures using Blackboard and Ecollege

- Courses taught – Management 101, Computers 101, Business 112, Entrepreneurship 110
  (Highlight the skills sought after in the announcement. Demonstrating effective use of technology is critical).

US Department of Labor, New Carrolton, MD
IT Assistant Director, (2005-Present)

- Manage staff of 25 IT professionals, develop policy and reports, counsel employees on tasks, training and promotion issues. Develop and deliver PowerPoint presentations for organization leadership. Conduct teleseminars, Skpe and instant message tutorials for IT users.
  (These details let hiring officials know he is skilled with internet technologies to conduct courses as well as present material to various audiences. It also includes common sought after terms used in online human resource systems)

Public Library, Arlington, VA
Volunteer Trainer, (2009-2010)

- Taught patrons how to use Microsoft Office through hands on training, lectures, webinars and PowerPoint presentations. Answered patron IT related questions, developed training manuals and handouts.
  (Even though this was not a paid position, it highlights training, customer service and technology skills. Non paid assignments count too.)

Additional Qualifications – any jobs, tasks, awards, qualifications, training that apply to the position

References – see attached *(Attach a list of 3 to 5 current references that include an address, telephone number and email for each person listed. Let your references know when you apply for jobs and who might be contacting them.)*

JOB CONTACT SHEET

DATE	ORGANIZATION	POINT OF CONTACT	CONTACT TYPE (call, email, resume, application system)	RESPONSE (Form letter, system note, call, email)	FOLLOW UP TYPE & DATE (email, call, interview, resubmission)

Resources

SCHOOLS WITH ONLINE PROGRAMS

A.T. Still University of Health Sciences
Abilene Christian University
Adams State College
Aiken Technical College
AIU online
American College of Education
American InterContinental University Online
American Military University
American Sentinel University
Ameritech College
Anna Maria College
Anthem College Online
Antonelli College
American Public University System
Arcadia University
Arizona State University
Arkansas State
Argosy University Online
Ashford University
Atlantic International University
Austin Peay University
Averett University
Bacone College
Baker College Online
Baker University

Barry University
Baton Rouge Community College
Bay Path College
Bay State College
Bellevue University
Benedictine University
Bethel University
Berkley College
Boise State University
Boston University
Bowling Green State University
Brandeis University
Brenau University
Brookline College
Bryant & Stratton College
Buena Vista University
California Coast University
California National University
California State University
California University of Pennsylvania
Capella University
Carroll Community College
Cecil College
Central Christian College
Central Pennsylvania College
Central Michigan University
Central Texas College
Chamberlain College of Nursing
Chancellor University
Chatham University
Chaplain College
Chesapeake College
The Chicago School of Professional Psychology
Clark State University
Cleveland Institute of Electronics
Cleveland State University

College of DuPage
College for Financial Planning
College of Southern Maryland
Colorado Christian University
Colorado State University
Colorado Technical University
Columbia Southern University
Concord Law School
Concordia University
Creighton University
Cumberland University
Daniel Webster College
DePaul University
DeSales University
DeVry University
Dominican University
Drexel University Online
Duquesne University
Eastern Kentucky University
eCornell
Eastern Kentucky University
ECPI University
Ellis University
Erikson Institute
Everest University Online
Everglades University
Fielding Graduate University
Florida Hospital College of Health Sciences
Florida International University
Florida Tech University Online
Fordham University
Fort Hays State University
Full Sail University
Gannon University
George Mason University
George Washington University

Georgetown University
Glion Institute of Higher Education
Gonzaga University
Graceland University
Graduate School USDA
Grand Canyon University
Gratham University
Gratz College
Harrison College
Hawaii Pacific University
Henley-Putnam University
Herzing University
Hodges University
Hope International University
Howard University
IIA College
Immaculata University
Independence University
Indiana Business College
Indiana State University
Indiana Tech
Indiana Wesleyan University
International Academy of Design and Technology
Iowa Central College Online
Ivy Bridge College
Jacksonville University
Jackson State University
Jones International University
Kaplan University
Keiser University
Keller Graduate School of Management
Kent State University
LA College Online
Lancaster Bible College
Lasell College
Lehigh University

Lesley University
LeTourneau University
Lewis University
Liberty University Online
Lincoln College Online
Loyola University
Lubbock Christian University
Malone University
Marist College
Marygrove College
Marylhurst University
McKinley College
Miami Dade College
Michigan Technical University
Mid-America Christian University
Minnesota School of Business
Minnesota State University
Mississippi Virtual Community College
Mountain State University
National Defense University
New England College
New England College of Business and Finance
NJIT
New York Chiropractic College
Northcentral University
Northeastern University College of Business
Northwestern College
Northwestern University
Norwich University
NDNU
NOVA Southeastern University
Ocean Online College
Ohio Christian University
Ohio University
Oregon Institute of Technology
Oregon State University

Our Lady of Lake University
Pacific Oaks College
Penn Foster College
Philadelphia University
PIMA Medical Institute
Pittsburgh Technical Institute
Portland State University
Post University Online
Purdue University
Rasmussen College
Regis University
Robert Morris University
Sacred Heart University
Saint Francis University
Saint Joseph's Online
Saint Leo University
Saint Mary's University
Saint Peters College
Saint Xavier University
Salem University Online
Schiller International University
Scott Victory University
South University
Southern New Hampshire University
Southwestern Christian University
St. Joseph's College
Stetson University
Strayer University
Sullivan University
Syracuse University University College
The Bush School
Thunderbird School of Global Management
Tiffin University
Ultimate Medial Academy
University of Massachusetts Online
University of Cincinnati

University of Florida
University of Illinois
University of Liverpool
University of Maryland Baltimore college
University of Maryland University College
University of Minnesota Crookston
University of Nebraska
University of New England
University of North Carolina
University of Phoenix
University of Pittsburgh
University of the Rockies
University of Saint Mary
University of San Francisco
University of the Sciences
University of Scranton
University of Southern California
University of the Southwest
University of Vermont
University of Washington Online
Upper Iowa University
Utica College
Vanderbilt School of Nursing
Vermont Law School
Victory University
Virginia College
Walden University
Waldorf College
Western Governors University
Western International University
Western New England College
Westwood College
Wisconsin Lutheran College[1]

---

1   List compiled using http://www.guidetoonlineschools.com/online-schools and
     http://www.elearners.com/colleges

Job Sites

---

http://www.academiccareers.com/
http://www.academploy.com/jobs.cfm
http://www.adjunctnation.com
http://www.adjunctprofessoronline.com/aggregator/categories/20
http://www.bilingualamerica.com/about/careers/
http://www.chronicle.com
http://www.connectionsacademy.com/careers/home.aspx
http://www.coursebridge.com/html/instructor_application.asp
http://www.Ed2go.com
http://www.edufire.com/why_teach
http://www.englishsolutions.ca/ces_jobs.php?set_
lang=en&myMeta%20=about.xml
http://www.extension.berkeley.edu/online/
http://www.facultyfinder.com/
http://www.facultyjobs-phoenix.com
http://www.gofluent.com/web/us
http://www.higheredjobs.com
http://www.higheredspace.com/
http://www.indeed.com/Online-Adjunct
http://www.indeed.com/virtual
http://www.insidehighered.com/career
http://www.k12.com/cava/who-we-are/career-opportunities/
http://www.onlineadjunctemploymentopportunities.com/
http://www.onlineadjunctjobs.net
http://www.onlineadjunctjobs.net/
http://www.scholarlyhires.com

http://www.scholarlyhires.com
http://www.tedjob.com
http://www.tellmemore.com/about/aboutus/careers/
http://www.tutorvista.com/teaching-jobs
http://www.virtualvocation.com
http://www.vu.ksurf.net/
http://www.wgu.edu/about_WGU/employment
https://www.careers-smarthinking.icims.com/jobs/intro
https://www.careers-smarthinking.icims.com/jobs/search?ss=1&searchKe
yword=&searchCategory
https://www.sh.webhire.com/public/737/
www.k12.com

ELearning, Training and Development Resources

Accordent – webcasts, media streaming
Adobe Captivate - elearning , screen capture, online trainings and quizzes
Articulate – authoring
Blackboard – education technology
Certpoint – elearning, LMS, talent management
Cornerstone on Demand – Talent, learning, performance management
Desire 2 Learn – LMS solutions
Digitalchalk – online training
Element K – learning solutions, online IT training
Epic – elearning, online and blended learning
Essential Skillz – online learning, LMS
Expretus - elearning
Faculte – collaborative video based learning
Intellego – elearning and application training
Line – elearning, blended learning
Kineo – elearning, training and LMS solutions
Knowledge Advisors – learning and talent management
Knowledge Factor – elearning, authoring
Meridian - LMS
Mindleaders – elearning programs
Nelsoncroom – elearning, professional exams
Plateau – talent management
Rapid Intake – elearning

Quick Lessons – collaborative elearning
Remote Learner – learning services
Saba - LMS
Skillsoft – elearning and It certification
Softchalk – elearning, authoring
Taleo – talent management software
TechSmith – screen capture, recording software
Thinkingcap - elearning
Trivantis – elearning, LMS
Webex – collaborative tool

Online Groups and Blogs

———◆·❈·◆———

LINKEDIN GROUPS

Able Adjuncts
Adjunct Professors/Instructors
Business Academia
College Textbook Authors
eLearn
ELT Professionals Around The World
Higher Education Teaching and Learning
How To Teach Online
Learn to Teach
Online Adjunct Professors
Online Adjunct Rolodex
Online Adjuncts Network
Online Educator
Online Faculty - Adjunct, Full-Time, University Administrators
Online professionals
Online Teaching
Online teaching
Technology-Using Professors
Text and Academic Authors Association
The Adjunct Network

FACEBOOK GROUPS

Adjunct World
Adjunct Faculty Community
Higher Education Teaching and Learning

Yahoo Groups

Online Adjuncts

Myspace Groups

Adjunct Experts

Blogs

http://adjunctprofessors.ning.com/

http://adjunctworld.blogspot.com/2011/06/this-weeks-online-adjunct-jobs-6311.html

http://blog.lib.umn.edu/tel/blog/2011/07/online-instructor-shares-best.html

http://community.elearners.com/all_blogs/the_elearners_news_blog/b/elearnersnews/archive/2006/06/13/So-You-Wanna-Teach-Online_3A00_-About-Becoming-an-Online-Instructor_2C00_-Part-II.aspx

http://gregaloha.wordpress.com/2011/03/16/prioritizing-online-instructor-roles/

http://onlineadjunctjobs.blogspot.com/

http://theonlineinstructor.blogspot.com/

http://thesabloggers.org/2008/01/faculty-ethics-on-facebook-the-collaborative-project/

http://www.onlinecollege.org/2011/06/08/follow-these-blogs-online-instructor-edition/

Online News

http://www.degreeinfo.com
http://www.elearners.com
http://www.facultyfocus.com/
http://www.geteducated.com
http://www.themoderndegree.com
http://www.universalclass.com/teachonline/
http://www.worldwidelearn.com
http://www:adjunctsuccess.net/index.php

Online Educator Training

Teaching Tutorials
http://www.teachertrainingvideos.com/blackboard/index.html

Distance Education offers a list of organizations with online teaching courses, programs and certificates.
http://www.distance-education.org/Degrees/Education-10/Teaching-50/

Blackboard Certification training
http://www.isb-me.com/isb/service_detail.asp?sr_id=12&menuid=subcat menu7&tdid=subcattd7&tdheight=75

The Learning House
http://learningcentral.learninghouse.com/
Has online education best practices and Moodle courses.
Contact training@learninghouse.com for additional information

Maryland Online has a certificate for online adjunct teaching (COAT).
http://marylandonline.org/coat/
Contact Bobbi Dubins (bdubins@allegany.edu), Project Director, for additional information

FacultyTraining.net has online instructor training course.
http://www.facultytraining.net/
Contact Mark Adams (madams@facultytraining.net) for additional information

Pearson eCollege: eTeaching Institute offers courses to learn about applications using the Pearson learningStudio (eCollege).
https://secure.ecollege.com/etch/index.learn?action

Indiana University School of Continuing Studies offers a certificate in Distance Education.
http://scs.indiana.edu/prof-programs/online/de-cert/index.shtml
For additional information, contact skglasgo@indiana.edu

University of Michigan offers an online instructor certificate program.
http://www.umflint.edu/oel/OIC.htm

LERN offers an online instructor certificate.
http://www.teachingonthenet.org/courses/certified_online_instructor/index.cfm

Stephen Austin University offers Blackboard and online instructor certification courses.
http://www.teachingonthenet.org/courses/certified_online_instructor/index.cfm

NC State University offers an online instructor certificate program.
http://www.coned.ncsu.edu/comprehensive.html

References

"Advantages of Working From Home Lure Staff, Employers." 16 August 2003. USAToday.com. 2 May 2011 <http://www.usatoday.com/tech/news/techinnovations/2003-08-16-telecommute_x.htm>.

Answer, The. Assaraf, John & Smith, Murray. New York: Atria Books, 2008.

Babb, Danielle and Jim Mirabella. Make Money Teaching Online. Hoboken: John Wiley and Sons, 2007.

Beals, Jeff. Self Marketing Power - Branding Yourself as a Business of One. Omaha: Keynote Publishing, 2008.

Bedford, L. "The Professional Adjunct: An Emerging Trend in Online Instruction." Online Journal of Distance Learning Administration (2009): 3-7.

Brainy Quote. 2012. 5 May 2011 <http://www.brainyquote.com/quotes/>.

"Bridges and Barriers Teaching Online College Courses Study." July 2007. The Sloan Consortium. 1 February 2011 <http://sloanconsortium.org/jaln/v11n2/bridges-and-barriers-teaching-online-college-courses-study-experienced-online-faculty-thi>.

Byrne, Rhonda. The Secret. Hillsboro: Beyond Words Publishing, 2006.

Canfield, J. and Hansen, M. The Aladdin Factor. New York: Berkley, 1995.

Canfield, Jack. The Success Principles: How To Get from Where You Are to Where You Want to Be. New York: Herper Collins, Inc., 2005.

"Community Reinvestment Act." 4 May 2011. <u>Board of Governers of the Federal Reserve System.</u> 3 January 2010 <http://www.federalreserve.gov/communitydev/cra_about.htm>.

Corbeil, J. and Corbeil, M. "Are You Ready for Mobile Learning." 30 November 2007. <u>Educational Quarterly Magazine.</u> June 8 2011 <http://www.educause.edu/EDUCAUSE+Quarterly/EDUCAUSEQuarterlyMagazineVolum/AreYouReadyforMobileLearning/157455>.

Dooley, Mike. <u>Manifesting Change. It Couldn't Be Better.</u> New York: Atria Books, 2010.

Dykman, C. and Davis, C. "Online Education Forum: Part Two - Teaching Online Versus Teaching Conventionally." <u>Journal of Information Systems Educations</u> (2009): 156-164.

"Essential Principles of High-Quality Online Teaching." 2003. <u>Southern Regional Education Board.</u> 3 February 2011 <http://info.sreb.org/programs/EdTech/pubs/PDF/Essential_Principles.pdf>.

Flood, T. <u>MBA Fundamentals of Business Writing.</u> New York: Kaplan, Inc., 2008.

Gawain, Shakti. <u>Creative Visualization, Use the Power of Your Imagination to Create What you Want in Your Life.</u> Novato: Nataraj Publishing, 2002.

Gibson, J., D. Tesone and C. Blackwell. "The Journey to Cyberspace: Reflections From Three Online Business Professors." <u>SAM Advanced Management Journal</u> (2001): 30-34.

Green, David. "Using Student Video Presentations in an Online Course." <u>Decision Sciences Journal of Innovative Education</u> July 2008: 521-526.

Greive, Donald. <u>A Handbook For Adjunct & Part Time Faculty & Teachers.</u> Ann Arbor: The Adjunct Advocate, 2003.

Gunter, Sherry Kinkoph. <u>Sams Teach Yourself Facebookin Ten Minutes.</u> New York: Pearson Education, 2011.

Haugh, Lee. "Writing a Teaching Philosophy Statement." March 1998. Center for Teaching Excellence, Iowa State University. 1 January 2011 <http://www.celt.iastate.edu/teaching/philosophy.html>.

Hering, Beth. "Getting Results." 28 06 2011. Career Builder.com. 22 June 2011 <http://www.careerbuilder.com/Article/CB-2415-Job-Search-Strategies-Getting-results-10-strategies-for-job-search-success/>.

Jeffers, Susan. Feel The Fear And Do It Anyway. Toronto, Canada: Random House, 1987.

Jones, T. "Institutional Support for the Virtual Professor." Turkish Online Journal of Distance Education (2004).

Lee, J. "Analysis of Essential Skills and Knowledge for Teaching Online." Association for Educational Communications and Technology (2004): 534-538.

Littlefield, Jamie. "How To Get a Job as an Online High School Teacher." 2011. About.com. 3 March 2011 <http://distancelearn.about.com/od/onlinecourses/a/Teaching-Online.htm>.

Lorenzetti, Jennifer Patterson. "Adjunct by Choice." 2011. Faculty Focus. 15 December 2011 <http://www.facultyfocus.com/articles/online-education/adjunct-by-choice-getting-past-the-stereotypes-of-online-instructors/>.

Maxwell, John. How Successful People Think. New York: Center Street , 2009.

Mayada, F. and J. and Bacsich, P. Bourne. "Online Education Today." August 2009. The Sloan Consortium. 1 December 2010 <http://sloanconsortium.org/jaln/v13n2/online-education-today>.

Meyer, Joyce. Power Thoughts. New York: Faith Words, 2010.

Miller, Chloe. "Focus On Adult Learning." 9 May 2011. Landing an Online Teaching Job. 1 August 2011 <http://hollymccracken.wordpress.com/2011/05/09/landing-online-teaching-jobs/>.

Myers, Ford R. Get the Job You Want Even When No One's Hiring. New Jersey: John Wiley & Sons, 2009.

—. Get The Job You Want Even When No Ones Hiring. Hoboken: John Wiley and Sons, 2009.

Pauley, Thomas and Penelope Pauley. I'm Rich Beyond My Wildest Dreams. New York: Berkely Publishing, 1999.

Pham, Alex. "Online Music Lessons Catch On." Miami Herald 25 January 2012: 8E.

Port, Michael. The Think Big Manefesto. New Jersey: John Wiley & Sons, Inc., 2009.

Proctor, Bob. It's Not About The Money. Canada: Burman Books, 2008.

Rao, Srikumar. Happiness at Work, Be Resilient, Motivated and Successful - No Matter What. New York: McGraw Hill, 2010.

ReCareered. 2011. 3 February 2011 <http://www.recareered.com/>.

Reichwald, Simon. "Simonreichwald.wordpress.com." June 2010. Simon Reichwald. 10 January 2011 <http://simonreichwald.wordpress.com/>.

Ringer, Robert. Million Dollar Habits. New York: Ballantine Books, 1991.

Rosenberg, P. "7 Ways To Ask For The Job At Interview's End." 16 March 2011. Simply Blog. 12 June 2011 <http://blog.simplyhired.com/2011/03/7-ways-to-ask-for-the-job-at-interviews-end.html>.

Schiffman, S. and K. and Geith, C. Vignare. "Why Do Higher Education Institutions Pursue Online Education." July 2007. Th Sloan Consortium. 1 February 2011 <Why Do Higher Education Institutions Pursue Online Education - Volume >.

Snow, Patrick. Creating Your Own Destiny. New Jersey: John Wiley & Sons, Inc., 2010.

Susan B. Wilson, Michael S. Dobson. Goal Setting. New York: American Management Association, 2008.

Terris, Ben. "Teaching Under Fire and Online From "Mortaritaville" In Iraq." 5 October 2009. Chronicle.com. 1 12 2010 <http://chronicle.com/article/Teaching-Online-From/48677/>.

Townsend, R. and Hauss, R. "The 2002 AHA-OAH Survey of Part Time and Adjunct Faculty." <u>American Historical Association</u> (2002).

"Understanding the Professional Online Adjunct." <u>Distance Education Report</u> (2010): 3,6.

unknown. "Internet Statistics." 2010. <u>Online Schools.</u> 20 November 2010 <http://www.onlineschools.org/blog/internet-stats/>.

VanSickle, J. "Making the Transition to Teaching Online: Strategies and Methods for the First Time Online Instructor." White Paper. 2003.

Vitale, J. and Wheeler, J. <u>Your Internet Cash Machine - The Insiders Guide to Marking Big Money Fast.</u> New Jersey: Wiley and Sons, 2008.

Vitale, Joe. <u>Hypnotic Writing, How to Seduce and Persuade Customers with Only Your Words.</u> Hoboken: John Wiley and Sons, 2007.

—. <u>The Key.</u> New Jersey: John Wiley and Sons, 2007.

<u>Writing a Teaching Philosophy, Iowa State University.</u> <http://www.celt. iastate.edu/teaching/philosophy.html>.

Young, Jeffrey. "In Case of Emergency, Break Tradition, Teach Online." 17 August 2009. <u>The Chronicle of Higher Education.</u> 23 April 2011 <http://chronicle.com/article/In-Case-of-Emergency-Break/48021/>.

Index